Praise for *The Blossom Method™*

'There are few books that can be called truly groundbreaking – this is one of them. Vivien Sabel shows parents how to communicate with their babies from day one. No more anxiety, frustration and confusion – just understanding and responding. Most importantly research shows that communicating with your baby makes a lifetime of difference supporting physical, emotional and cognitive development. A must read for EVERY new parent.'
Dr Rosina McAlpine, Associate Professor, The University of Sydney, Australia, founder of Inspired Children

'Ever uttered the words "What do you want?" in frustration to your crying, irritable or fractious baby? Well never again! Vivien Sabel outlines the many different, non-verbal but clear-cut clues to your baby's physical and emotional needs. Pay attention and you'll set the scene for a lifetime of enhanced intuitive response, communication and relationship.'
Janette Roberts, pharmacist, clinical nutritionist, pioneer in promo ⸻ *author o* ⸻ *ealthy Babies s* ⸻

'If you've ever been frustrated by your inability to interpret your baby's wants and needs, this book is for you. Vivien Sabel introduces The Blossom Method™, a revolutionary technique for reading your baby's body language. The results: less frustration, a closer parent/child bond, and much more parenting confidence!'
Susan M. Heim, co-author of Boosting Your Baby's Brain Power

'A valuable book for all parents wanting to form a long-lasting connection with their children. By following The Blossom Method™ parents will be able to understand and communicate with their baby from day one.'
Claire Marketos BA Psych (Hons), HDipEd, founder of Inspired Parenting, parenting/educational consultant

'We all know that babies cry when they're in distress, and as parents we come to recognise many of our own child's particular signs and signals, but what if babies are trying to communicate with us at a much deeper level, and because we don't realise that we fail to understand them? In this groundbreaking book Vivien Sabel's exciting and astounding discoveries open up a whole new world to bringing up happy, contented infants through her simple

method of Observing, Mirroring, and Responding – The Blossom Method™. This book is exciting because it will take non-verbal communication to a new level and challenge us to explore more fully the messages our babies are trying to tell us!'
Sue Atkins, parenting expert, broadcaster, speaker and best-selling author of Raising Happy Children for Dummies

'At seven days old we have already had a breakthrough using The Blossom Method™. And now we are using it all the time. We are becoming more familiar with her tongue patterns and we know we will discover so much more. I have read the book from start to finish. I couldn't put it down. It's life-changing.'
Sarah Spiers, new mother to Olive

'Vivien brings a unique perspective to the whole mother–child bonding relationship in its formative stages. This is a fascinating insight into what we can learn as parents and professionals about subtle communication with our babies right from birth.'
Rosalind Arden, former lecturer in psychotherapy, Leeds Metropolitan University

'Would you like to enhance your understanding of the non-verbal communication between you and your baby? The Blossom Method™ is an enjoyable, accessible support "tool" for anyone to use. The author's own story of being mothered and mothering, as well as the birth and parenting story in her heart-warming case studies, really bring Vivien Sabel's concept of baby-body-talk to life.'
Adela Stockton, doula/doula educator, author of Gentle Birth Companions: Doulas Serving Humanity

'*The Blossom Method™* by Vivien Sabel is an absolute gift. I highly recommend it to all parents or anyone who works with or has an interest in the positive development of our children. I was promised an easy to understand and apply method of developing the most amazing and enjoyable relationship with my child and I wasn't disappointed. In fact, through her fascinating and astounding discoveries, Sabel helps us all to enable our children to develop a deep sense of self and enrich their mental health and wellbeing.'
Heather Bestel, child therapist

'An interesting, inspiring and enlightening book that every new parent really should read. Vivien's passion for her subject is evident throughout and left me wanting to

learn much more about the subject of non-verbal communication between babies and parents. *The Blossom Method*™ is a must-read for all who want to further their understanding of the world of a baby. I think you have made a really important discovery here. I want more! A TV series and a DVD!'
Victoria Dawson is an author, consultant, trainer and sleep practitioner

'It's a nice strong "how to" – easy to read and experience for oneself. The Blossom Method™ is a simple three-step concept that allows for lots of personal adaptation. I enjoyed it. A great way to "read" your child as an open book (observe), "come to your senses" (mirror) and be "response-able" (respond). It is totally in sync with what I encourage in "learning partnerships" between parents and their children. This is indeed an example of leadership in action from the home tribe! Well done, Viv!'
Dr Yvonne Sum, author of Intentional Parenting *and leadership coach*

'I have read *The Blossom Method*™ and found it really clear and easy to read. I learnt a lot about "real" communication.'
Dr Minae Inahara

'This book is a jewel. A rare combination of practical techniques and research. If we all attended to pre-language communication in this way our whole lives would be clearer and more fulfilled.'
Julie Fawcett, business psychologist and executive coach, BA, DMS, FIPD, FRSA

The Blossom Method™

The Revolutionary Way to Communicate with Your Baby from Birth

Vivien Sabel

Vermilion
LONDON

1 3 5 7 9 10 8 6 4 2

Published in 2012 by Vermilion, an imprint of Ebury Publishing
Ebury Publishing is a Random House Group company

The Random House Group Limited Reg. No. 954009
Addresses for companies within the Random House Group can be found at
www.randomhouse.co.uk

A CIP catalogue record for this book is available from the British Library

The Random House Group Limited supports the Forest Stewardship Council (FSC®), the
leading international forest certification organisation. Our books carrying the FSC label are
printed on FSC® certified paper. FSC is the only forest certification scheme endorsed by the
leading environmental organisations, including Greenpeace. Our paper procurement policy
can be found at www.randomhouse.co.uk/environment

Printed and bound by CPI Group (UK) Ltd, Croydon, CR0 4YY

ISBN 9780091947538

Copies are available at special rates for bulk orders. Contact the sales development team on 020 7840 8487 for more information.

To buy books by your favourite authors and register for offers,
visit www.randomhouse.co.uk

Picture credits
All illustrations © Toby Clarke, ClarkevanMeurs Design Limited, except for:
Pages 74, 75, 80, 85 and 93: © Juliet Percival, www.julietpercival.co.uk;
Pages 119–122: © 2012 Cath Smith – BSL sign graphics – the LET'S SIGN Series –
www.DeafBooks.co.uk

All photography © Emma Hammond, www.dalesviewphotography.co.uk, except for:
Page 146: © Kate Abbey, www.kateabbey.co.uk

The information in this book has been compiled by way of general guidance in relation to
the specific subjects addressed, but is not a substitute and not to be relied on for medical,
healthcare, pharmaceutical or other professional advice on specific circumstances and in
specific locations. Please consult your GP before changing, stopping or starting any medical treatment. So far as the author is aware the information given is correct and up to date
as at January 2012. Practice, laws and regulations all change, and the reader should obtain
up-to-date professional advice on any such issues. The author and publishers disclaim, as
far as the law allows, any liability arising directly or indirectly from the use, or misuse, of the
information contained in this book.

To Vuyo, Blossom and Mum

Contents

Disclaimer

The Blossom Method™ can be used to recognise
some signs of illness, but if you have any concerns
about your baby's health always seek medical
advice from your doctor.

Foreword

Every new parent wonders how they will understand what the little person in front of them wants, needs, desires and feels, and what each cry, posture and movement indicates. I have met many families in my work as a speech language pathologist and all of them would benefit from learning how to communicate with their babies effectively. Whether the child is developing in a typical manner, has been born prematurely or demonstrates other medical or developmental concerns, the needs are similar for every family. In my professional work I haven't always had the answers but I have encouraged parents to become careful observers, responders and shapers of behaviour. Like Vivien, I have researched many theories and methods but have always relied more on my own intuition, experiences and education. The Blossom Method™ is by far the easiest and most sound method I have experienced, and the fact that it is suitable for *all* babies and their families means I am very excited about introducing it to those who want assistance in communicating with their babies.

This groundbreaking book outlines exactly how parents can read and develop their baby's non-verbal communication skills to increase the child's wellbeing and the parent's self-confidence, thereby allowing for a deeper bond to take place between parent and baby. This bond lays a firm foundation for future communication and cognitive skills. Vivien Sabel teaches parents how to communicate with their baby by carefully observing non-verbal behaviour and then mirroring and shaping these movements into functional communication.

By using these methods, parents can begin 'talking' with their babies in the first days of life. This book is for parents who want to be able to respond more readily to their baby's attempts to communicate. Parents are often cautious, lack confidence or feel left in the wings watching someone else become the 'expert' with their baby, something that can be particularly true for those with premature babies or those with medical or developmental concerns early in life. By using The Blossom Method™, parents can begin to take an active part in their baby's care and development with confidence.

Jennifer M. Hatfield, MHS, CCC/SLP
Speech Language Pathologist
President, Therapy and Learning Services, Inc.

Introduction

A baby starts talking from the moment she takes her first breath. A child's instinct for survival and human interaction drives her to communicate with her caregivers using unique movements, facial expressions, sounds, and mouth, lip and tongue shapes. Many of these go unnoticed in the early days of parenthood as everything focuses on providing the newborn with nourishment and comfort. After years of research involving parents and their children, I have mapped the behaviour of the babies I have worked with, including my own, and discovered a phenomenon that has never before been recognised.

Conversing with Your Newborn

As well as all the usual movements, signs and sounds that a baby makes in an effort to communicate how she feels, the shapes she makes with her tongue relate to very specific requests. It is possible to hear a baby's 'words', but only if you are 'listening'.

In this book I will introduce you to my revolutionary technique, The Blossom Method™, which will not only give you the skills to understand the language of the newborn but will also show you how to talk back so that your baby feels understood. Named after my own daughter, Blossom, who provided me with my first experience of tongue-talking, the term also echoes the blossoming relationship between adult and child during those early hours, days and weeks of life.

A World Without Words

My research began when Blossom was born in 2004, but the knowledge and skills that enabled me to develop my communication techniques with my baby were instilled in me from an early age. I was brought up by a profoundly deaf mother and learnt from a very early age how to communicate without words. I grew up with a heightened sensitivity to the significance of actions and expressions and often sensed my mum's frustration at not being fully understood by those around her, observing fleeting moments of distress in the tiniest movement of her eyes. My memories of my mother's parenting were based around not *what* she said but *how* she looked at me or how she moved her body. The power of her non-verbal communication was (and still is) immense. Being raised by a deaf mother and a hearing father has gifted me with so much, but it has heightened my sensitivity to both verbal and non-verbal language. The power of words and indeed the power of non-verbal language are incredible.

My mother tends not to use sign language to communicate. She mainly lip reads and uses body and facial expressions to relay messages to me. In turn, I communicate with her in the same way. As I work and live with the unspoken word, communicating in a non-verbal way is very familiar to me. I see in an instant when body utterances match spoken words and, conversely, when someone's body language says something different to the words they are using.

I now realise that my communication with my mum was, and still is, different to many others. She, like many of her deaf peers, relies on getting a message across in a direct fashion. I very much like this way of communicating. As a child it seemed a little bizarre that non-deaf people chose to communicate using so many words to convey a simple utterance. In British culture we seem to use flowery language to convey messages and sometimes it seems we skirt around the edges of our utterances, occasionally implying rather than simply saying it as it is.

When I was growing up, I only needed to glance at my mum to elicit information with regard to her well-being: her emotional self, her mood, her level of satisfaction, her state of health and even her level of hunger! This, of course, was a two-way process; my mum could elicit all of the above information by simply observing me. This made it possible to be and feel seen. Both mine and my mother's feelings and emotions appeared like words on our faces and bodies. For this reason, we were never really able to hide our true feelings from each other.

I can recall as a child an occasion when my mum met a casual acquaintance. This person spoke quickly, and I knew that my mother had missed much of what was said. My mother declared her deafness and, on doing so, the acquaintance began to over-exaggerate her lip patterns and words. My mum appeared saddened, ashamed and angry by this response – these feelings were written into her facial expressions and body language and are still unforgettable for me. During my childhood this was the only time I heard my mum *own* her deafness. Why would she if this was the way she experienced the responses of others to declaring her deafness? From that day forward I embraced my mum's deafness and tried to understand more about our differences. This supported our relationship and its development.

I think it was this relationship with my mother that

aided my developing interest in baby communication. Interestingly, neither my mum nor I recognised this as our primary communication system. I have only become aware of it in recent years following my experience of motherhood and my clinical training. I think it is because of my experiences with my mother that I tend to instinctively observe the body language of others. I believe I have been doing this all of my life, just as Blossom seemingly does it too. I use this skill in my work as a psychotherapist. I do this with everyone I have a relationship with. My friends tell me it's impossible to hide anything from me! I do, however, believe that this skill is not exclusive to me, hence my desire to share it with you and your babies for the benefit of all. I believe we all have the capacity to understand and develop an understanding of non-verbal communication.

As an example, consider the eyes. The eyes can provide you with so very much information. If they are moist, they may be telling you that this person is upset. If they are cold they may represent an absence – a lack of emotion. I believe you will all recognise sadness in the eyes of another. You will also know the look of happiness, whereas the lower jaw and the upper lip can provide clues to unhappiness, distress and upset.

I believe body language skills and the observation of facial expressions can be a skill that is developed over time.

Once you've accessed the most obvious of expressions you will soon become acquainted with the less obvious. It does, however, take time to observe and to deepen the development of these skills.

Understanding Non-verbal Communication

When Blossom was born, I instinctively studied her body language as minutely as I had been accustomed to doing with my mother. All parents are fascinated by their newborns, and my husband and I were no different. We watched Blossom's facial expressions and tongue, mouth and lip movements closely, and, because non-verbal communication has played such a vital role in my own life, it was these movements that I responded to rather than the sounds my daughter made. I was fascinated by this tiny creature in front of me and amazed at how much she was trying to tell me even in the first few days and weeks of her life.

Soon after Blossom's birth I became aware that her facial expressions, and especially the movements of her tongue, mouth and lips, were far more sophisticated and complex than I had realised. Movements which could have seemed random were, in fact, far more specific, and each had its own meaning. I realised that if I could learn what they meant, I could have a much closer level of communication, and a fuller understanding of what Blossom was trying to tell me.

I began to feel confident that I could 'read' my baby and understand her visual messages. According to the position and shape of her tongue and other non-verbal messages, I felt I could determine her needs, matters in relation to her health, and the level of her excitement or distress. Even more importantly, I was picking up on these signs and reacting to them before Blossom even felt the need to cry. As a new mum, I was happy that, even though she was still so young, I could understand what my daughter was telling me, and I was relieved that she was not frustrated. Instinctively I began to mirror back Blossom's mouth and body movements. Incredibly, as I mirrored her tongue-pushing or mouth shapes, she did it back more.

By studying Blossom's movements, tongue shapes and expressions carefully, I was soon able to attribute specific meanings to each one. I quickly learnt to detect in advance when she was about to cry, fill her nappy or even become unwell. I discovered that I could predict when illness was starting up to 36 hours before she showed any physical symptoms. Between us we developed a wonderful early communication system. Who said babies can't talk?!

I believe that because I used The Blossom Method™, Blossom was a very happy baby and was confident in her request making. She felt comfortable and secure as a result of having her needs met. For example, I would have known her nappy was full, even before she had finished, by observing her tongue movements – her 'tongue-talking' (see page 16). I could then prepare to change her nappy in advance. If I missed her tongue-talking, I would quickly note any non-verbal expressions of discomfort and be able to change her nappy way before she reached the crying stage. In seeing her windy expressions, I would mirror back her expression, indicating to her that I knew what she was experiencing and then I would swiftly move in to relieve her of her wind. I believe meeting her needs so quickly stopped her from having to resort to crying. The level of communication I was developing with Blossom enabled me to respond to her needs in a way that would not otherwise have been possible, but the real power of The Blossom Method™ was in making it possible for me to show Blossom that she was being listened to, and this had many positive benefits for her health and wellbeing (see Chapter 2 for further information on the benefits The Blossom Method™ can bring).

When Blossom was just a few weeks old I attended a local 'Parent & Toddler' group and upon arrival I introduced Blossom and myself. In my enthusiasm I asked how the parents were all getting on with understanding their babies' non-verbal communication and tongue-talking. I was genuinely surprised to be met with a sea of blank faces. It was clear that they didn't know what I was talking about. I honestly thought that they were all doing what I was doing. I just simply assumed that all parents were addressing their babies' non-verbal clues and cues to aid them to meet their needs before they reached the crying stage, just as I had understood my mother through her non-verbal communication and I understood my daughter through hers. I suppose I was surprised by these findings and knew then that this story was worth sharing. I am still friendly with many of these mothers now. They have all been very enthusiastic about The Blossom Method™ and in me sharing my story with you.

Start Talking

This book is designed for all mums, dads, all carers of babies, students of life or otherwise, and all who have a passion for learning about non-verbal communication and the potential of early communication systems. It is designed to support a new way of parenting, one that will have a positive impact on your baby and therefore you as a parent. It will also help anyone involved in the care of babies to enjoy improved understanding and communication to enhance the lives of others.

You and your child will benefit from this book, but developing an understanding of non-verbal expressions, body language and facial expressions applies to your relationship with yourself and with others. You will begin to realise how much can be gleaned non-verbally. This is a gift – a gift you and your baby will enjoy and benefit from.

I believe my methods will help you develop your own unique and individual relationship with your baby, one that is not affected by any negative experiences you may have experienced when being parented.

I have come across many babycare and parenting books over the years and some of them have left me feeling 'not good enough' as a parent. My intent here is different: I want to provide you with useful 'tools' to benefit you and your family. This book has been written for your enjoyment and learning, and to support you in your desire to be good enough.

The quotes gathered for the body of this book have come from parents, many of whom are professionals and experts in their own fields.

'The Blossom Method™ gave me the confidence to parent in a way that felt right and natural to me. Unlike some other books, it didn't make me feel patronised or that I was "doing it wrong".' – Sarah, mother to five-week-old baby Olive

The feedback about *The Blossom Method*™ I have received from both parents and professionals has been nothing less than sensational – described as *groundbreaking, astounding, revolutionary, amazing, original, innovative* and much more.

Preparing the Way

I would encourage all parents to read this book before their baby arrives. It is so helpful to understand all about the method and its benefits. The Blossom Method™ has successfully been introduced to parents whose babies haven't been born, are just born, or are a few days old, a few weeks old or who are already several weeks or even months old, but understanding the concept during pregnancy allows parents to start observing expressions and tongue, lip and mouth movements from the moment of birth.

Using This Book

You may want to read the book through once before you begin using The Blossom Method™. Chapter 1 outlines the method and its essential techniques – how to observe, mirror and respond to your baby. Chapter 2 covers the many benefits of the method to you and your baby. Chapter 3 explains how to begin using The Blossom Method™ with your baby. Chapter 4 targets particular areas such as hunger, tiredness, discomfort, frustration, toileting issues and illness, and shows you how to use The Blossom Method™ to recognise and respond to these before they cause your baby any distress. In Chapter 5 you can discover how baby signing can benefit your baby and how The Blossom Method™ can make the transition to baby signing smoother.

I hope you enjoy learning about The Blossom Method™ and the many benefits it can bring to you and your baby.

Vivien

Please note: Throughout the book I've alternated the gender of the baby chapter by chapter.

CHAPTER 1

What is
The Blossom Method™?

In researching baby communication, and in particular The Blossom Method™, I became fascinated by the many ways in which babies express themselves without verbalising. When I talk about baby communication, most people think I am referring to babies' sounds, such as cooing, crying and gurgling; however, reading babies' body language allows us to interpret our babies much further. The bodies, facial expressions and even tongue, lip and mouth movements of our babies can help us understand what they are experiencing long before they reach the crying stage. We can learn when they are going to fill their nappies, have a desire to eat, how hungry they are, if they are in distress, have wind (therefore a degree of discomfort), are experiencing deeper discomfort (for example, reflux), appear lonely (isolated and as a result in distress), over-stimulated, under-stimulated and frustrated. In-depth understanding will deepen your knowledge of *all* that is *your* baby.

With The Blossom Method™ you can observe, mirror and respond to your baby *from the minute he is born*. To maximise the potential for communication, it is ideal to read this book when you are pregnant so you can start these techniques as soon as your baby is born; however, you won't be disadvantaged if you begin using The Blossom Method™ at a later stage. Simply begin as soon as you can. Whether it is your first or fifth child, read it and try it. You have nothing to lose and so much to gain! If you access this book after the first three months of your baby's life, then do not worry. I have worked with babies after the 12-week period and, although I have noted less use of tongue-talking, they are still very responsive. My daughter is now six years old and I still use the principles – I observe, mir-ror non-verbally (as well as verbally) and respond to meet her needs. I believe this further enhances and deepens our communication. I often make verbal enquiries into what I observe in her facial expressions and body language. She also uses verbal language to describe feelings. She will talk about tingling in her tummy or fuzziness in her head, and from these body observations we are able to elicit much in terms of how she is feeling and what she is experiencing. She is in tune with both her body and her mind.

A baby will continue to use his tongue, but other verbal language will take over any time from five months onwards. I will talk more about other forms of baby communication, such as the transition from The Blossom Method™ to baby signing (communicating with your baby through simple sign language), a little later (see Chapter 5).

Observe, Mirror and Respond

The Blossom Method™ uses a simple three-step approach of Observing, Mirroring and Responding. First of all you should take plenty of time to **observe** your baby. Notice the movements of his tongue, lips and mouth. In doing so, recognise any specific needs associated with these movements. Look for any other facial expressions and body language. The next stage involves **mirroring** what you have observed to show your baby that you have 'heard' what has been said. Finally, you **respond** to your baby's 'words', reassuring him that he has been understood and is participating in a two-way dialogue. With The Blossom Method™ you *follow your baby's lead*. He teaches you what he is seeking – to be seen, heard and understood. *You* are learning *his* language. The Blossom Method™ is a multi-sensory activity. By introducing the concepts of observing, mirroring and responding, I am encouraging you to communicate with your baby wholly.

Observing

Use your skills of observation to see, touch, sense, hear, smell and wholly experience your baby. What do you notice intuitively when you focus on his face and body? The more you observe, the more you will learn. What is your baby showing you? Your baby's hunger can been seen in his mouth and lip movements. Your baby's wind can be seen on the bottom lip and facial expressions – for example, a fullness seen in the lower lip and sometimes a look of discomfort in the face and eyes. Observation over time will encourage a deep understanding of your baby's moods, desires and needs.

As well as observing your baby's body language and facial expressions, The Blossom Method™ pays particular attention to the mouth and tongue. Tongue-talking has become a way for me to describe a feature noted in all the babies I have worked with. It is particularly apparent in those under 12 weeks. In the first

'It was very interesting to observe my baby's frequent tongue movements and realise she was trying to communicate her needs at just a few weeks old.' – Beverley and her 10-week-old baby girl

weeks of life, babies use their tongue, mouth and lips to make requests of their parents and to advise their parents of what they are experiencing, and in Chapters 3 and 4 I give you many in-depth examples of these.

> 'Observing my newborn is amazing, but learning more about what she is saying through her facial expressions is incredible.' – Laura and her five-week-old baby girl

Mirroring

Mirroring, a unique and important element of The Blossom Method™, is a simple activity that requires you to look at your baby and simply mirror back his expressions and body language. If you gaze lovingly towards him, he will instinctively mirror your gaze. When you mirror your baby's actions, you are also *confirming* and *affirming*. As a parent you are likely to be the first mirror in and of your baby's life. I view non-verbal mirroring as similar to using 'baby-talk', also known as 'motherese' and most recently 'parentese' (the 'baby talk' many people naturally use when speaking to a baby). Mirroring may feel a little strange at first, but persevere as the non-verbal communication between you and your baby will be amazing.

I have been asked if I felt self-conscious in my mirroring of Blossom. I didn't, but I understand that some people may feel self-conscious. If so, mirror when and where you feel comfortable. Some of this mirroring may be easier for you in the comfort of your own home, but I would encourage you to communicate in this way as often as possible in the first six months of your baby's life.

Here are some simple examples of mirroring: if you see your baby's tongue moving in and out of his mouth, simply copy this action and mirror it back. Your baby will repeat what you have mirrored. You can then mirror it back again. As you become skilled in mirroring, you will develop an awareness of what this tongue movement means to your baby. For example, if your baby makes an 'O' shape with his lips and mouth, make this shape with your lips and mouth. He will mirror it back to you and eventually you will begin to develop an understanding of what this expression means. If your baby's eyelids are drooping in tiredness, simply mirror his eye-drooping back to him. Your baby is telling you he is tired and in mirroring you are telling him you understand that he is tired and you are encouraging him to sleep. If your baby is wincing in discomfort with wind or a bowel movement, simply mirror this expression back. Your baby will know you have acknowledged what he is experiencing and it

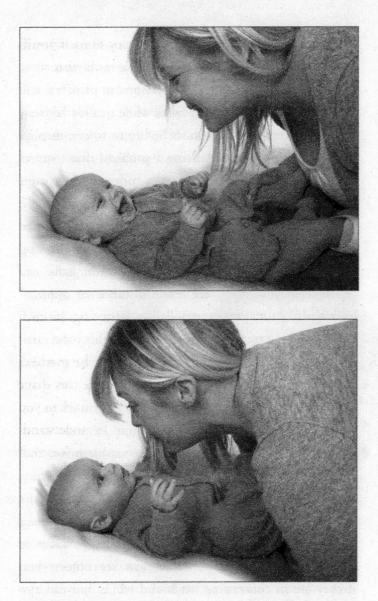

Cat mirroring the mouth and eye patterns of her baby, Sebastian

will encourage him to continue expressing himself. It will also help him to bring up wind or move his bowels.

If your baby looks uncomfortable and in pain, it is still valuable to mirror his expressions while quickly addressing his discomfort and pain. If he begins to cry, then he may be unwell or experiencing a problem that requires medical assistance. If you have any concerns about your baby's health, always seek medical assistance immediately.

In the early days, you will need to be positioned fairly close to your baby for him to see your mirroring actions. A newborn baby can see to a distance of approximately 8–10 in (20–25 cm). This is roughly the distance between the mother's breast and face, so your baby can see you when you cradle him in your arms. Your baby is attentive, too, and curious about your face. Research has shown that babies are more interested in pictures of faces than an image of a random pattern, and they prefer happy faces to unhappy ones! Newborn babies can see objects best if they are in contrasting black and white, but can also distinguish bright, primary colours.

'My baby's lips looked full and she winced in discomfort. I mirrored back these expressions and my baby repeated them back to me. In no time at all she had brought up her wind.'
– Marie and her four-week-old baby girl

Here are some of the benefits of mirroring:

- It confirms and affirms.
- It helps your baby to feel 'heard' and seen.
- Using mirroring can relieve issues such as constipation, wind, discomfort, hunger, thirst, frustration, under-stimulation, over-stimulation and the need for 'contact'.
- It stimulates a baby's brain activity.
- It helps your baby to learn about you and himself.
- It will help you to learn all about your baby's communication.
- It helps you to bond with your baby.
- Mirroring is a wonderful way for grandparents to bond with their grandchild.

Mirroring is mainly done subconsciously. Tune in and mirror consciously to support the development of your very own communication system. As you observe and begin to mirror your baby, he will begin to know, feel and experience your love and, as a result, feel secure and grow in confidence. Your baby has an innate drive to communicate and deeply connect with you. This can begin with joyful observation and, importantly,

'I love seeing my baby's reactions to me mirroring her movements.'
– Peter and his six-week-old baby girl

Using Parentese

As well as mirroring and responding, using 'parentese' (see above) with your newborn will help him to become familiar with particular words, such as Dada, Mama and his own name. I believe this is most important in the early months of life. When you begin to recognise your baby's attempts to use words, it is most useful to respond with normal language, rather than 'parentese'. You are once again providing a mirror, but this time it is a verbal mirror. Blossom started to speak clearly at five months old. We stopped used 'parentese' at this point and used our natural speaking voices for her to develop her speech normally. Her speech developed quickly and she hasn't stopped nattering since!

mirroring. The mirroring of your baby will develop his knowledge of you, himself and his world.

Mirroring helps your baby to acquire body language skills, body awareness and body confidence. Through the process of mirroring, he will develop an awareness of mimicking, imitation and echoing. By echoing the experience of your baby and subsequently responding to the non-verbal or verbal utterances, you can support him to feel seen and therefore heard.

I was careful to let Blossom know she was being listened to and understood. She learnt to 'hear' me through my mirroring of her. In mirroring back I was trying to understand what she was telling me. I instinctively copied or mirrored in order to 'make sense' of or process her non-verbal expression. My mirror was a repeating and processing exercise as well as one of acknowledgement and affirmation. It is similar to repeating what another has said in order to try to understand it.

After I mirrored back the tongue patterns to Blossom, she consistently mirrored them back to me. We continued to 'play' with this mirroring pattern, and then, once I had discovered how to interpret her tongue patterns, I

Mirroring: a Natural Form of Communication

Mirroring is a valuable resource we can tap into naturally. It is used in psychotherapy and in sign language interpreting. Non-verbal mirroring will support a deaf person to access more information in relation to what is being said and how it is being stated. In interpreting it is essential to mirror accurately; this allows us to develop accuracy skills and helps us to understand more about feelings, emotions and personality. In psychotherapy mirroring both verbally and non-verbally is used to help clients to feel both seen and heard. Non-verbal communication relies on the listener responding visually to acknowledge that the other person has been 'heard'.

responded to her needs by making myself available to her. In my research I've found that babies appear to notice quickly that you are mirroring them. Initially they appear curious but soon after it becomes part of everyday communication. If you are available to mirror often, your baby seemingly uses his non-verbal utterances, such as tongue-talking and mouth movements, more often.

Responding

Responding positively to what your baby experiences and expresses will help him to feel nurtured and more secure. Responding to your observations after mirroring your baby's non-verbal 'language' (tongue, lip or mouth pattern, and so on) will help you to explore what he is looking for. Is he hungry? If so, you respond by giving him the breast or bottle. Is he bored? You respond by stimulating him in some way. Is he in discomfort? You respond by exploring what might be wrong with him and taking action to relieve any discomfort. These questions and many more can be explored using The Blossom Method™. In Chapter 4 you will discover how to use The Blossom Method™

'My favourite part of The Blossom Method™ is mirroring Joe's mouth movements.' – Vicki and her 18-week-old baby boy

to respond to specific needs, such as hunger, illness and discomfort.

How you respond will be very much dependent upon how you have been responded to in your infancy and beyond. As parents we are bringing our own history of the way we were parented to our own parenting, and I feel it's important to recognise this before we act out the same patterns without thought. It is ideal if we can do this before becoming parents, but if that's not possible you can look to change your behaviour at any time.

Dr Rosina McAlpine, founder of Inspired Children, says, 'When we first become parents, generally all we really know about parenting is the model handed down to us by our own parents – good or bad. Regardless of whether we feel we had a good, bad or somewhere in between parenting experience, we can choose to accept that our parents did the best they could with the level of knowledge, understanding and skills they had in relation to parenting.

'One of the things I am really enjoying is mimicking the sounds, while copying the tongue movements. Rose also seems to enjoy this. I often say "I love you" to Rose during these "chats" and she responds by making slowly the same sounds – I feel this further bonds us.' – Martin and his 13-week-old baby girl

We also need to accept that how well we were parented determines the basic level of skill that we start out with as parents ourselves. So, unless at some time we have made a conscious effort to learn a new model of parenting and have been successful in putting the new model into action, our experience of being parented is how we subsequently parent. This happens despite our best intentions.'

It is not easy to explain why this happens, and this could easily be the subject for a whole other book! It is fair to say it is complicated and the effects of our own experience of being parented become part of who we are. Our children embody all of their experiences, including their experience of our parenting. Dr McAlpine says, 'They absorb everything uncensored from their environment, including their experience of parenting. These parenting experiences become recorded or programmed in their subconscious, only to be retrieved and replayed subconsciously in the future once they have their own children.'

Regardless of the way you were parented, your knowledge and insight here will give you power. Even though your experience of being parented will subconsciously be part of who you are, your personality will support you to make a choice.

The Blossom Method™ will encourage you to do something positively different! It is likely you will not have experienced The Blossom Method™ in your own childhood

Body Confidence

I can recall many years ago observing a young mother and her baby. She was changing her baby's nappy. The young mother was clearly disgusted by the content of her baby's soiled nappy. The look of horror was presented both verbally and non-verbally. If she responded consistently in this way, displaying negative responses to normal bodily functions, even at this stage in infancy it is likely that her baby would have picked up on her negativity and anxiety. We can but wonder how this mother's negative expressions may have impacted upon her baby. I wonder if her baby grew to feel ashamed of his bowel movements? Perhaps as a child he might have begun to 'hold on to' his bowel movements as a result of experiencing shame.

In contrast I have seen many mothers and fathers changing nappies laughing and making funny faces with their babies. I have heard these parents using verbal expressions such as 'Poo, that's a smelly nappy!' These parents have a look of joy upon their faces and they are clearly enjoying all of what is their baby – smelly nappies too! I believe we can benefit from seeing the positive in our babies' experiences of their bodies, and by responding to them with joy we teach them from infancy that their 'normal' functioning and their bodies are nothing to be ashamed of. This will help your child to be body confident. This body confidence will continue into childhood and adulthood.

experience, so begin with this and watch your baby develop his communication skills with you.

By becoming more aware of how you respond to your baby, you will understand how this may have a lasting impact on him. If your baby feels he is being responded to, then he will be more likely to communicate. If you are as present and responsive as you can be, then this will help your baby to develop his communication skills.

By taking the time now to look at how you respond verbally and non-verbally to your baby, you are considering the benefits of positive non-verbal and verbal expressions. If you are able to be as present as possible and are able to respond supportively and positively, then this will

'With The Blossom Method™ the onus is on me to get to know my baby, not on general information or by teaching my baby how to demand things from me. I like that it is non-verbal and natural. Most non-verbal methods of communication rely on the parent teaching their child to ask or respond in some way. The Blossom Method™ is natural and demands only that a parent pay some extra attention and promote the continued use of the natural cues provided by your baby.' – Charlene and her 11-week-old baby son

go a long way to making your baby feel self-assured and self-confident.

You can see how by using The Blossom Method™ you are giving your baby a more immediate response. It allows you to 'tune in to' your baby and meet his needs and in doing so encourages a deepening of the relationship between both of you. Your understanding will encourage satisfaction and comfort. This will be mirrored back to you and then in turn back to your baby. And so the happiness continues …

Your observation will be the key to your success; your mirroring will be both fun and interesting; your response will depend on developing your observational skills and how much you place faith and trust in yourself as a parent and your baby as a provider of much information. Your baby is providing you with all you need. It will be your job to observe his offerings, mirror his eye-gaze, smiles, blinking, and tongue, lip and mouth patterns, and then respond to his needs or desires. The Blossom Method™ is baby-led parenting and parenting with consciousness for the 21st century!

CHAPTER 2

Why Use
The Blossom Method™?

How many times have you heard a parent say to a crying baby, 'What is it? What's wrong? Why are you crying? Is it your nappy? Are you hungry? You're so tired.' Frustration is felt by both carer and child. The baby is desperate to be understood and the desire of the parent to find out how to soothe the child can be overwhelming. Medical conditions, illness and anxiety can deepen that sense of anguish and create difficulties that can have a negative impact on the parent–child relationship during those formative early months. This is where The Blossom Method™ is so effective.

By using The Blossom Method™ we knew when our daughter, Blossom, was hungry or thirsty. Each tongue-talking expression was provided in advance of the action or request – some shapes minutes before and some seconds before, but all with consistency, all repeated and mirrored back until Blossom's needs were met. All of the tongue-talking expressions were presented with other information that would allow us to glean more about Blossom's feelings and emotions relating to the above actions and requests. If, for example, Blossom experienced a degree of pain or some discomfort, this information was usually presented on her face, and sometimes on her body, but always in addition to her tongue-talking. We knew when she was constipated. We knew well in advance when she was going to move her bowels or urinate. There is a great deal of value in developing this level of understanding of your baby's needs.

Getting to Know Your Baby

If we agree that it is important to understand emotions, isn't it a good idea to take more time to consciously observe the emotions of our babies by looking at their facial expressions, reflexes, responses, tongue-talking and body language? We sometimes miss non-verbal utterances as we wait to hear verbal language and crying.

If you know what your baby is experiencing and what emotions are behind this, you can help her more than you had anticipated. You can help her feel less anxious, which will make you feel calmer and more relaxed with your baby. You can observe the body language and facial expressions of your baby well in advance of hearing her cries. I believe 'tuning in' to your baby in this way and the development of your early communication system will promote happiness in your baby and therefore you.

Observing your baby, attempting to understand all that is said and mirroring back the utterances not only creates yours and your baby's very own primal and early communication system, it can alleviate the many anxieties of a new parent. In feeling less anxious, you will project less of your anxiety on to your child and create a more positive environment for nurturing.

I met with a first-time mother, Helen, and her six-week-old baby, Rosie, and introduced them to The Blossom Method™. Rosie was using her tongue and I encouraged Helen to mirror back her movements. Rosie was initially curious and then she was full of joy as her mummy continued to mirror her. Rosie was lying in her cot, and as Helen mirrored her Rosie raised her arms and legs in excitement. Rosie then presented us with a beaming smile. She was overjoyed by this experience and we were delighted to have experienced her joy. Helen was fascinated by Rosie's response. Helen said that as a result of learning all about The Blossom Method™ she has thoroughly enjoyed mirroring Rosie and, as a result, learning all about Rosie's non-verbal communication.

If you have knowledge of The Blossom Method™ prior to birth, it means you will start to recognise some of your baby's signs and signals in relation to her needs from the very first days of her life. I believe we either miss the non-verbal expressions or we take this information in without realising it.

Facial expressions allow us to read more about what our babies are experiencing on an emotional level. The following recent experience may provide you with some insight into non-verbal observation.

I recently observed a mother and her 14-week-old baby. Initially the baby slept, but as soon as the baby woke up and was taken out of her pram, her expression was one of both shock and surprise. Her little facial expressions and body language demonstrated a true reflection of what this baby had experienced. When she left her home with her mummy she was placed in a pram and only saw her mother's face. As the mother pushed the pram, her baby fell asleep. The mother was then joined by a friend, and then by me and my daughter, in a café. When the baby opened her eyes she was in an unfamiliar setting with some unfamiliar faces. Her

expression was telling us she was puzzled, a little con-
fused, curious, but not overly afraid. If she could have
spoken, I sense her questions would have been some-
thing along the lines of: 'Where am I? How did I get
here? Who are these people?' Her expression also told us
she was both shocked (but apparently not in an overly
negative way) and surprised. So the baby's expression
seemingly blended a number of emotions, including
an element of fear and a sense of puzzlement. Her eyes
widened, her eyebrows were raised with a slight frown,
her arms moved up and down (which for me meant
there was more to her expression than simple surprise).
I decided I would use baby signing to 'speak' to her.
Babies are born with a desire to communicate. They
will experience baby signing as communication and
will want to join in immediately! I looked at the baby
and both said and signed, 'Where's Mama?' The baby's

'Reading *The Blossom Method™* before my baby arrived really supported me to think more about my baby's body language and to know what to look for. It made me feel more confident to know I was on the right track.' – Gill and her two-week-old baby girl

*eye-gaze shifted from me to her mummy. I repeated the
actions and words and the baby repeatedly turned her
head and eye-gaze towards her mummy.*

Easing Frustration and Distress

Babies can easily become distressed and cry. Crying is one
of the first verbal expressions you may hear from your
baby. She may have let out a primal cry once she made
contact with the outside world. She may have experienced
great joy and comfort in the womb and may want to cry
upon leaving you and her 'mummy tummy'. In the first
instance her cry will be the only form of verbal expression
that will stimulate you and your primal parental response.

Initially you may not notice any differences between
your baby's cries, but after a while of getting to know each
other you may be able to distinguish between them. If
your baby lets out a piercing cry, she may be in pain. As
you comfort her, her crying may subside. If the crying
doesn't subside, then it is likely she is still experiencing
pain. Your baby may cry when she has a bowel movement
or has urinated, or when she is constipated or has wind.
If your baby is shocked or experiences pain, is hungry
or thirsty, is isolated, is over-stimulated, under-stimulated
or tired, she may resort to crying to verbally express her

discomfort. Imagine if you could predict with confidence your baby's hunger, wind, constipation, tiredness, a need for contact or otherwise, before your baby feels the need to cry; this could mean so much to you and your baby. I could predict these things with my daughter, and using The Blossom Method™ so have many others. This said, you may not have instant success using The Blossom Method™ and it may not work for you every time. You may be having an off day, you may be feeling unwell or you simply may not be as tuned in as you have been. Therefore even using The Blossom Method™ your baby may cry and become frustrated. This is fine. Be patient and keep your feelings of anxiousness to a minimum. It can take time and practice to master The Blossom Method™, but it will become easier in time. Most of all, enjoy it! This time with your little one cannot be recaptured. Use The Blossom Method™ to have fun with your baby!

Understanding your baby's non-verbal utterances will decrease the need for her to resort to crying. She will, however, continue to experiment with her vocal chords and 'play' using her voice.

In working alongside many parents and their babies, I was able to help them discover their babies' signs for constipation, wind, thirst, tiredness, over-stimulation, under-stimulation, frustration and hunger. For example, babies Olive and Sebastian both used a strained smile for wind and constipation. Using The Blossom Method™ core principles of **observation**, **mirroring** and **responding** really helped here. The parents **observed** their babies' expressions and **mirroring** them back encouraged the babies to echo their original movement, which they then mirrored back to their parents. It was the repeating and echoing of their original expression that seemingly encouraged the babies to release their wind. In observing and hearing the wind both sets of parents knew they had been able to support their baby with this. Once understood, these expressions would support the parents to create additional solutions to the problems of wind and constipation, such as patting and rubbing. In addition to mirroring back, I also pointed out to the parents the body language signs of wind and constipation (taut tummy, arched back, protruding tongue, wriggling in discomfort, full bottom lip – see page 84 in Chapter 4). This deepened their knowledge of their own babies' communication.

I noted baby Joe's 'O' shape to indicate his search for the breast and hunger. His mum Vicki enjoyed mirroring

> 'We are very interested in the method and are trying to implement it. Richard seems to be better tuned in to it than me and we find one of our twins slightly easier to "read".' – Claire and Richard and their six-week-old twins

this back to him and responding by providing him with a feed. At 18 weeks, Joe now uses the 'O' expression to request a feed from his mother. Claire and Richard used The Blossom Method™ to spot non-verbal signs in their twins and discovered that one of them was easier to 'read' than the other.

You won't always be available to observe your baby: no doubt you will have many other calls on your time, such as other children, and work or home responsibilities. I'm simply encouraging you to remember and to learn about your baby's non-verbal clues and cues as they will help you and your baby to experience a deep connectedness, a deeper relationship and an even more wonderful bond. Your baby will cry, and this is fine, but it is lovely to know that you are following your baby's teachings and that in doing so she is guiding you to meet her needs through her own language and communication.

'When I found out I was pregnant I was so very excited. I had always worried about understanding my baby. How would I know what she was saying? In speaking to Vivien about The Blossom Method™ I began to feel less anxious about understanding my baby.' – Lisa, 25 weeks pregnant with her first baby

Improved Communication

Not all babies communicate in the same way, but my observations of babies during the early hours, days, weeks and months of life have established common patterns of behaviour. These can be interpreted by parents and caregivers and provide a powerful insight into the emotions and needs of the child.

By using The Blossom Method™ technique of observe, mirror and respond, you can create an effective early communication system. The Blossom Method™ will make you more aware of your baby's efforts at communication and thereby allow you to connect more deeply with her. Conversing with your baby from such an early age will help her to feel and experience trust and to develop confidence in her relationships with you and others. If your

'I believe that communication is key to parenting on a physical and emotional level. A child who is aware of her own emotions and is emotionally articulate can build life-long rewarding relationships – and more importantly build self-confidence. Close parental communication is key to this.'
– Sarah, mother of two

baby feels understood, contained and seen (and therefore heard), this will give her strong foundations for her emotional and physical development. A much greater level of communication is possible between babies and their parents or carers than we are accustomed to expect. Babies whose messages are understood begin life feeling less frustration and more attuned, and are consequently more likely to be happy and secure. In feeling and experiencing security and happiness in infancy they are provided with a solid foundation for good future mental health and wellbeing. So the benefits of The Blossom Method™ go well beyond babyhood.

'In using The Blossom Method™ I feel more confident about knowing what my baby wants and needs and I feel more connected to my baby because I feel like we understand each other more deeply than before.' – Charlene and her 11-week-old baby boy

Continual observation, mirroring and response will lead to language development between you and your baby. The conversation is dual communication, with both sides acutely aware that they are being listened to and understood. Mutually understanding creates a sense of calm and reassurance and forms the basis for a strong and rewarding relationship that will continue to develop as your baby grows and adds to her range of communication tools.

Bonding

Think about what is being created in the space between you and your baby as you interact. Reflect on your own experience of being parented and acknowledge that there are elements of this history that you will be bringing to your own parenting technique (see page 25). Focusing strongly on your emotions and your influences as you bond with your baby will help you to attune with her more powerfully and respond in a deeply personal way to her non-verbal and verbal utterances. As you tune in to your baby's sensations, needs, feelings and desires through observation, mirroring back and responding, notice what happens to the bond between you.

Using The Blossom Method™ will encourage the development of the foundation of your bond from day one! It will promote positive learning and communication in a safe and natural way. You are co-creating an early communication system that is baby-led and parent-centred.

Creating an Environment for Growth

Offering a secure and nourishing environment for your child can help her to develop greater creativity, confidence and intelligence. Children show huge levels of determination as they work towards their first words and those initial shaky steps across the room. They watch the adults around them and mirror their behaviour in an evolutionary process that enables them to progress from baby to toddler and beyond. Parents naturally encourage them to progress from crawling to walking and from babbling to speaking, but what if that encouragement began even earlier? With The Blossom Method™ your baby experiences encouragement and understanding from the moment she is born.

'Information regarding the very exciting Blossom Method™ was forwarded to me by my baby signing teacher – I thought it sounded great. On the basis of the information gleaned I spent some time with Rose, mirroring back her tongue movements – my observation has been that Rose becomes very animated and excited. Similarly, my husband has also found that Rose appears to engage in this interaction and we both get a sense that she feels we are talking to her and that we understand her.' – Kathy, Martin and their eight-week-old baby girl

Brain Development

While in the womb babies' brains are already significantly developed, but, once your little bundle of joy arrives, using The Blossom Method™ will help to positively stimulate her and further support the development of neural pathways in her brain.

At birth most of your baby's brain cells will already be formed, but most of the connections among the cells are made during infancy and childhood. Early contact, positive communication and interaction with the environment (you as parents and other caregivers) are most critical in a child's brain development. This contact will help the building of neural pathways and connectors required for language development, empathy and intellect.

If we consider a baby's brain as a work in progress, we must also consider how the outside world shapes its development through how we respond as parents. Love and nurture, the provision of varied, interesting and stimulating experiences, physical activity, positive nutrition and peaceful sleep all help it to develop further. The nurturing environment of your baby will support and shape brain development as she uses all her senses – vision, touch, taste, hearing and smell.

Deborah McNelis, a baby and child expert from America, discovered through her research that babies benefit from experiencing loving interactions and from having their needs met by loving, responsive parents. 'Your baby's early experiences form their foundation. Your baby will learn what to expect, they will learn more about themselves, how to relate to and with others and how to self-regulate. These experiences will support your baby to understand more about themselves, their world and the relationship with others. If as parents we are able to consistently respond to our baby's expressed needs we are giving our babies the capacity to develop powerful brain connections that will ultimately lead to both healthy emotional development and optimal learning.'

I have witnessed first-hand the success of using The Blossom Method™. My own daughter, Blossom, had clear speech from five months old. I understood her non-verbally and I believe she understood me from the first few weeks of her life. Blossom at age five was also recognised as being gifted and talented in the areas of literacy and communication. Many psychologists have suggested that a child's grasp of language may affect her intelligence. If this is the case, then using The Blossom Method™ is likely to help optimise brain activity.

Research has shown that consistently responding to the needs of a baby can have an impact on her ability to form healthy relationships with others, to problem-solve, to have empathy for others, to tolerate the frustration of failure, to have more patience, to calm down from excitement. A baby whose needs are consistently met may also have a longer attention span, be able to better manage physical reactions to emotions, have greater skills in communicating emotions in healthy ways, feel less anxiety, exhibit fewer behavioural problems, have more confidence and a positive self-perception, be less fearful and have more willingness to explore and learn through challenges.

I believe that your response to your baby's body language promotes more body language awareness in your baby. As you and your baby become more conscious about her or her body communication, it will help in early development of frontal lobe brain function. The frontal lobes are considered to be the centre of our emotional world and the 'home' of our personality. The frontal lobes are involved in language, memory, initiation, problem-solving, motor function, judgement, social behaviours and impulse control. The left frontal lobe is said to be involved in language-related movement and the right frontal lobe is said to be associated with non-verbal attunement or abilities.

A Happy Baby and a Happy You

A beaming smile, sparkling eyes and giggling are all outward signs of contentment and happiness in a baby. Words we commonly use to describe ourselves when we feel happy include excited, satisfied, content, relieved, affirmed, at peace, smiling inside and out. Whichever words you use to describe happiness, these utterances can be found in your baby's body language and facial expressions. Through the process of developing your observational skills, and absorbing on a multi-sensory level all that you see, hear, touch and smell, your awareness will develop and, as a result, you will learn more about yourself, your own body language and your communication with your baby and others. In improving body-to-body connections between yourself as a parent and your baby, you will improve your own mind–body connections.

When children are very happy we recognise this in their expressions. Their eyes, eyebrows and lips will all show signs of happiness just as they did hunger and tiredness. By observing these non-verbal signs we can gain reassurance that our child is content and mirror back our satisfaction.

This happiness is co-created and experienced between parent and child and provides a wonderful foundation for a flourishing and mutually nourishing relationship. When babies experience unhappiness and their needs remain unseen, and therefore unheard, they may develop distorted perceptions. Early memories form the foundation of our emotional life and if that foundation is solid it will lead to confidence in managing emotional experiences in childhood and beyond. There is more than enough evidence both in psychotherapy practice and beyond that provides us with no doubt that positive early baby experiences lead us to seek out positive adult experiences.

Understanding more will also help you to decode your baby's body language and will help you to meet your baby's needs. By having her needs met through The Blossom Method™, your baby will feel cared for. The caring shown will be experienced by her and subsequently seen in her facial expressions and body language. You will pick up on her verbal and non-verbal utterances and this will allow you to experience your happy baby. This will no doubt promote your happiness and reduce any anxieties you may be experiencing. Your happiness will then be presented naturally in your face and mirrored back to your baby. In addition to non-verbal mirroring, if you also talk to your baby she will experience the happiness and soothing tone in your voice in addition to experiencing your positive body language and affirming facial expressions.

Considering my experiences and what I have demonstrated in my findings, Blossom was indeed a very happy baby, who seemingly experienced a deep-seated sense of connectedness with me as her mother. She also has the most amazing relationship with her father. By using The

Blossom Method™, you too can bring great happiness to your baby and yourself.

The chapters that follow will show you what to look for in your baby's expressions, tongue, mouth and lip movements, and body language. You will learn how to respond to allow frustration to be replaced by understanding and a deep sense of security.

CHAPTER 3

Using The Blossom Method™

As a parent you will have marvelled at your wonderful newborn. You will have noted things like the colour of your baby's eyes, his smell, and the look and feel of his skin and hair. From the minute your baby is born you will no doubt find yourself looking and listening in an attempt to understand what your baby wants and needs. These observations are, I suspect, made instinctively and we observe, at least most of the time, almost without noticing.

Look beyond the beauty of your newborn and listen with your eyes. Through this process you will see and hear so much more. You

'What's surprised me about The Blossom Method™ is that it *really* works from day one!'
– Nicola and her six-week-old baby boy

will note different expressions and, in particular, mouth and tongue movements. I advise you to undertake these observations from the day your baby is born. You will be shown them immediately, so why not access them immediately?

Body Language

A baby's body language is incredible. Why not break away from the book now and simply spend time looking at your baby's facial expressions and movements? He will provide you with information from his eyes and his gaze, and the movement of his mouth, lips and tongue. Your baby will provide further information with his hands, arms, feet and legs. Body movements are used slightly differently by each individual, whether that person is a baby or an adult. It is only by observing your baby that you will be able to determine what he is trying to communicate with these movements.

Arm and leg movements

One example of body language is a baby's arm and leg movements. Some babies use their arms to communicate, but others make very little expressive arm movement.

Arm movements are particularly useful in determining a baby's needs from the age of approximately 10 weeks. This said, I have noted in many babies, even just a week or so old, the raising of the hands to the mouth to explore. Once you have observed these movements, let your baby know you have 'seen' and therefore 'heard' his experience through mirroring his arm movements. What's interesting to me about this is I have seen parents doing this in what seems to be an unconscious way. I want you to be aware and conscious of these non-verbal expressions in order for you to communicate and understand each other more and at an earlier stage. In my research I have observed the leg movements of many babies. I have seen babies move their legs in excitement – usually a fast, gentle kicking movement. I have also seen babies move their legs in discomfort, with both wind and soiled nappies. The level of the individual discomfort means that each display has varied slightly. Some babies have moved their legs with determination, bending at the knee as if climbing invisible stairs! Other babies have pushed their legs out, keeping them as

'I know when my baby girl has had enough and wants to be put down because she repeatedly straightens her back. When she wants you to pick her up, she pushes her tummy forward and arches her back.'
– Pete and his 19-week-old baby girl

straight as possible. Just keep an eye out for *your* baby's leg movements. Once you've noted them, look at your baby's facial expressions and other body language. You will soon understand whether your baby is in distress or is full of excitement and joy.

Newborn reflexes

In the first hours, days and weeks of their life, newborn babies display certain natural reflexes – their first body language! It can be useful to understand what these reflexes mean.

- **The Moro or Startle Reflex:** This reflex causes the baby to extend his arms, legs and fingers and arch his back. The reflex occurs when a baby is startled by a loud noise or other stimulus, or if he feels that he is falling.

- **The Grasp or Palmar Reflex:** If as a parent you place your finger into your newborn's palm, he will grasp it. If you attempt to release your finger, your baby will continue to grasp. The grip of a newborn is strong and steadfast.

- **The Plantar Reflex:** This is tested at birth by the attending midwife. As a parent you can test this yourself. Just simply stroke the sole of your baby's foot from heel to toe and watch him as his toes spread upwards and his feet turn in slightly. As your baby grows, his response changes – from 6–18 months his toes will no longer flare but will curl downwards.

- **The Rooting Reflex:** This is where we see your baby responding to touch or stroking on the cheek. He will respond by turning his head and 'puckering up' for a feed. If you wish to see this for yourself, simply stroke your baby's cheek and watch him turn his head and prepare himself for a feed.

- **The Sucking Reflex:** This is triggered by something making contact with your baby's mouth. If you gently place your knuckle into your baby's mouth, the sucking reflex will be encouraged.

- **The Stepping Reflex:** This is a fascinating reflex. If you place your hands under the arms of your baby, then hold him away from you and place his feet on a solid surface, he will begin to step. It will look like your baby is attempting to walk. Although this reflex is said to disappear after a couple of months, it will reappear when your baby is ready to take his first steps.

Facial Expressions

In early infancy, much can be seen on the face, in the eyes and in particular the mouth, lips and tongue of your baby. The mouth, lips and tongue shapes are being provided for a reason. In the first stages of infancy these are the patterns I want you to pay close attention to. These are the movements you will notice immediately (literally from the minute your baby is born) and these are the patterns you can mirror back with relative ease.

Make a mental note of what you see, then mirror back or mimic the expression (the pouting lips, the tongue protruding and simultaneously gliding across the lower lip from left to right, the smile, the blinking of the eyes) and respond accordingly by addressing the needs of your baby. Initially having made a mental note of your observations, respond by investigating your baby's nappy, his hunger needs, his need for a cuddle, to be winded or to sleep.

Eye-scanning and eye-gazing

Your baby will scan with his eyes, in search of the breast, other sources of food, contact, comfort and physical connection with you as his primary caregiver. Your baby will scan for unknown visual delights with some sense of puzzlement, just as we may when we gaze upon the excitement of the unknown or inexperienced. When you look into the eyes of your adult loved ones, what do you see? Do you see a sparkle? An element of sadness? A look of anger? A sense of pain? A picture of happiness? This in relation to babies is no different. The 'windows' of your baby's soul will provide you with much information too. Take a look at your baby now. Is he pleased to see your smiling face? Is he excited? Is he distracted or uncomfortable? Is his body moving or still? Is he puzzled? Is he relaxed or does he look like he is experiencing discomfort? Is he searching and scanning or gazing happily?

If your baby is satisfied and happy, he will meet your gaze and remain with your gaze. If he is seeking something in addition to your gaze, then he will not remain in eye contact with you. If he avoids your eye-gaze, could it be he is potentially over-stimulated? Your baby's eyes will give you so many clues. What are your baby's eyes telling you?

You may wish to create your own baby body language interpretations and add to the ones I have identfied for you. What are your baby's eyes telling

'I have learnt to watch for his cues, allowing him to find his own routine that has been baby-led, free from crying and even enhanced his sleep patterns.' – Sarah and her six-week-old baby boy

you about how he feels? **Observe**, **mirror** and **respond** here too. You can mirror the gaze, the scanning, blinking and drooping eyelids as well. When Blossom was over-stimulated she would move her head from side to side, as if she was telling me, 'No, mummy, I don't want you to do that!' When I mirrored her blinking, she very much enjoyed it. I can recall the smiles and laughter to this day.

Understanding Your Baby

In focusing on body language and facial expressions you will be shown in advance – before he cries – the needs of your baby. You will start to recognise some of your baby's signs and signals and notice how they correlate to his needs. You will quickly start to develop your observations and, as a result, tune in to your baby. He can tell you all that you need to know. You simply need to believe in yourself and be open to witnessing his expressions.

'Charlie can wake me up with the sound of licking his lips rather than angry wails! He is happier – so am I.' – Deborah and her six-week-old baby boy

When Blossom was just a few days old I was carrying her and 'talking' to her. I would introduce her verbally and non-verbally (through sights, sounds, smells and touch) to her world and mine. I remember carrying her close as I prepared a meal for myself and my husband. I introduced her to the ingredients and she responded to them with facial expressions. I held a small piece of onion, garlic and some carrot and allowed her to experience the smell, sight and touch of the ingredients. The facial expressions allowed me to understand more about how she experienced these food items. In 'experiencing' the onion and garlic, she winced and blinked her eyes. These were obviously powerful in her experience. Blossom seemed to 'embrace' all of her world and when she felt over-stimulated she would let me know by moving her head back and shaking it from side to side.

Tongue-talking

The concept of 'tongue-talking' is truly unique. I have seen the consistent use of tongue-talking in all of the babies I have had the privilege of working and spending time with. Tongue-talking is the way in which your baby uses his tongue to explore his world and communicate with you. Watch carefully as in the early months your baby will use his tongue much of the time – so often in fact that you may almost take it for granted. Your baby's tongue will move in and out of his mouth; he will push it out, pull it back in, slide it across his lips, use it to explore his hands and your breast or bottle. For a baby, the tongue is like an extension to the senses – something your baby uses to experience his world.

Very early on I noticed Blossom's tongue movements, which were so active. I became curious about what her different tongue shapes meant. And after a few days I saw that many of these were consistent and repeated at the same times, coinciding with specific needs. Some meant hunger, others meant searching, some were directly connected to bodily functions and others related to emotional needs. When Blossom was seeking closeness and physical contact, her tongue seemed to be gently protruding, as if she was 'looking' for me with her tongue. When she was hungry, her tongue was rounded and soft, and she would poke it in and out with increasing speed and effort, according to the degree of hunger. I also began to recognise other tongue patterns that indicated bowel movements, wind and the passing of urine. The urine and bowel movement tongues were more pointed than the others. The urine tongue (which I have noted in other babies too) curls in at the sides. Within just a few weeks I had understood all of her non-verbal messages.

I initially began to mirror back Blossom's tongue activity with some sort of subconscious, primal instinct in the hope that Blossom would recognise that, by being seen, she was being 'heard' and understood.

In Chapter 4 I will take you through the common tongue shapes demonstrated by babies and explain what your baby is trying to tell you when he makes these shapes. In very early infancy the tongue and mouth patterns seem to be similar for all babies, but the other non-verbal expressions they display may provide you with different meanings for your baby.

Look out for particular tongue movements in your baby. Following your observation, begin to mirror the tongue pattern. For example, look for 'the hungry tongue' – the soft, rounded, tongue that protrudes in and out of your baby's mouth when he is hungry. Your task is to simply mirror it back to him. See what happens. Your baby will repeat the tongue, lip or mouth pattern back to you. Practise this for a minute or so and place your breast or bottle near him. He will guide you as to whether he is hungry or not.

Sometimes a baby uses tongue-talking in combination with other facial expressions. When your baby is searching for something, such as your breast, he might scan with his eyes at the same time as he 'talks' with his tongue. As the tongue moves from right to left and back again, observe your baby's eye-gaze and discover what it is he is searching for. Your baby's eye-scanning will offer you further clues as to what he is looking for. You will begin to recognise patterns in his behaviour and in doing so understand when he is over- or under-stimulated. As you become aware of the different tongue patterns, simply **mirror** them back to your baby. Once you have mirrored the tongue back to him, you can assess his needs. He may require a feed. If so ensure you offer your breast or a bottle to see if this is what he is searching for. The searching tongue is likely to be a search for food, comfort, contact and communication. Engage your baby in communication as this is what he wants to do from the minute he is born.

Practice makes perfect

As you develop your skills and you continually respond to your baby's needs using The Blossom Method™, you will find that his confidence in using the tongue, mouth and lips will develop and grow. The more you share in relation to **observing**, **mirroring** and **responding**, the more your baby will use the tongue, mouth and lips as a primary form of communication. As you become more practised you may find that your baby cries less. He will, of course, want to experiment with his vocal chords and will want to experience more of the noises he can make, but minimising the need to cry can only be a good thing.

Sarah (and Peter), like all of the parents who have explored The Blossom Method™, have shown significant enthusiasm and have offered their time and energy freely to learn more about their baby's communication. In meeting Sarah in the early phases of my research and while she was pregnant, we were able to spend many hours together.

Sarah had been introduced to the concepts of The Blossom Method™ and tongue-talking prior to the birth of her daughter. She therefore felt confident in her observations and noticed her baby's tongue-talking and body language signs immediately. She appeared to be self-assured in what she was looking for and she was delighted with the benefits of understanding her baby non-verbally. Sarah literally couldn't wait to get started. She encouraged her husband Peter to get involved too.

Sarah felt reading this book prior to having a baby and understanding the benefits of The Blossom Method™ are important. Sarah and Peter felt knowing what to look for and embracing the mirroring concept supported Olive well. Before the arrival of baby Olive, Sarah felt she knew exactly what to look for and this helped her to experience increased skills and confidence with The Blossom Method™. Increasing your confidence will support you to minimise your anxiety and meet your baby's needs before he reaches the crying stage.

Sarah, Peter and Olive had their first breakthrough using *The Blossom Method*™ when Olive was just seven days old. Olive was a very windy baby and often after feeding she looked pretty uncomfortable for some time. One night Olive's dad, Peter, observed and then mirrored one of the facial expressions she used when she had wind. She mirrored it back to him, and each time she did the face she repeated it back and at the same time she was able to pass wind. It was like she was forgetting how to push the air out and her doing it with him really helped her to focus.

Olive's use of her tongue was noticeable immediately. Some of the other babies I have worked with have used their tongues less. Other babies have used their mouths and lips more. Olive's tongue was so active; it moved in and out and Sarah mirrored it back to her and she mirrored it back to Sarah. Sarah then responded by seeing if Olive wanted a feed and she latched on immediately. Even at two weeks old Sarah was able to see when Olive was hungry and was able to determine her level of hunger, just from her tongue-talking.

Sarah went on to learn which breast Olive would prefer by the direction she pointed her tongue (see page 84. When Sarah tried to give Olive the 'wrong' breast, she wouldn't latch on.

In meeting with baby Olive at four weeks old I was delighted to see Sarah and Olive in their wonderful dance of attunement. Olive was a contented baby. She appeared to be gratified, settled and responsive. The Blossom Method™ had introduced Sarah and Peter to the concepts of baby body language, tongue-talking, observation, mirroring and responding. Sarah appeared very confident in her mothering skills and she said that The Blossom Method™ had helped her to develop this body awareness and wonderful confidence.

Alternatives to Visual Observation

Observing in the ways outlined above may be difficult for caregivers with a visual impairment or where cultural conventions make it impractical. Observation uses all the senses and can be practised through the careful monitoring of sounds, smell, touch and an intuitive sense of what is being communicated. Just as every baby is unique, so too is every parent and The Blossom Method™ therefore lends itself to being adapted to the needs and preferences of those implementing it.

The smell of your baby's breath

Blossom's breath has a glue-like quality some 24–36 hours before she comes down with something. It has been present since her birth and still remains to this day. Smelling her breath has always been a good indicator of ill health in Blossom.

'I remember this smell on my baby's breath with my first born but it never happened with my other baby. It was easy to know with my eldest that she was under the weather.'
– Jane, mother of two grown children

'My baby's breath smells different today. It usually smells of milk but today it smells weird. I wonder if he's going to be ill?'
– Aisha and her four-week-old baby boy

'My baby's breath had the characteristic sweet/sour smell of milk most of the time, but when he was under the weather his breath smelt like glue. I could always tell when he was going to be ill by the scent of his breath.' – Juliet and her 14-week-old baby boy

Breathing

When your baby is born, he will begin to breathe automatically. The rhythm of your baby's breathing may be variable up until the age of approximately 26 weeks. Observe and listen to his breathing and become attuned to what is 'normal'. He may begin to experiment with his breath and breathing, puffing and panting and enjoying the different noises and sensations experienced while experimenting with these newfound abilities. Your baby's breathing will vary at different points during sleep; this will be dependent upon what stage of sleep he is experiencing.

Self-soothing

Self-soothing can be seen in adults and stems from early experiences. You will all know someone who uses self-soothing. They may not be aware of it themselves. I observe this on a daily basis in my psychotherapy practice. I am able to see people rubbing their legs, hugging themselves, rubbing their ears, gently biting at their lips, stroking their cheeks, and many, many more examples can be noted in all humans. These non-verbal actions are usually initiated unconsciously and are unconsciously experienced as soothing.

Self-soothing is a natural repetition of an earlier experience. Your baby was comforted and rhythmically soothed when he began life in the womb. During pregnancy the mother provides a safe haven and a home for the baby, during which time he begins to experience comfort, holding and the rhythm of life – the soporific sound of your heartbeat as his own life blossoms inside of you. At this stage your baby will only recognise the pleasure and comfort derived from such an experience. He will not see himself as separate from you. He will see himself as you. He will not be able to differentiate between what is you and what is himself. Providing all is well in the womb, once born he will naturally seek to recreate this early experience. His instinct here is symbolic of his power to know what it is he is seeking to re-experience. Put simply, he knows what it is he likes and instinctively knows how to recreate it.

Once born, the soothing environment is recreated externally and is provided by you and found through skin-to-skin contact, your loving embrace, soothing voice, non-verbal expressions of love, wonderment and your loving gaze. These expressions will be seen, felt, experienced, heard and embodied by your baby.

Use The Blossom Method™ to observe, mirror and respond to your baby's self-soothing techniques. For example, if he is rubbing his ear, use the back of your hand to gently rub your own ear. If he is rubbing his eye, you can rub your eyes. If he is touching his face, you can touch your face and you can intermittently touch his face too, rub his eye or rub his ear. Take care with this and always be gentle, using the back of your hand and taking care not to scratch him. In mirroring his self-soothing techniques, your baby will know that you have 'heard' and understood him. He may mirror them back to you.

The mirroring of such experiences will provide your baby with a wonderful opportunity to learn about what it is he needs to soothe himself. As a primary caregiver you are your baby's teacher; he is instinctively learning these skills from you and will go on to develop his own methods of self-soothing. Self-soothing techniques are many and varied; they include stroking, rubbing, rocking, rhythmic movement and sucking. If you see your baby self-soothing, then recognise the evolutionary cycle that has occurred.

Here are some specific self-soothing movements:

- **Rubbing ears** – usually means sleepiness or may simply mean self-soothing to promote sleep.
- **Sucking fingers/hands** – recreating a sucking motion is simple self-soothing or possibly indicates hunger.
- **Hands on cheek or face** – recreating skin-to-skin contact feelings and an exploration of self.
- **Rubbing or stroking** – recreation of the skin-to-skin contact between mother and baby.

- **Rhythmic, repetitive or rocking movement** – re-symbolises the experience of life in the womb. This is a self-soothing technique to induce feelings of comfort.

Your Body Language

Your body language and the way you respond to your baby non-verbally are important too. I think we can learn about our babies' preferences from how we hold ourselves and our babies. If you are anxious and your stance is rigid and stiff, then your baby will experience this in the way you are holding him. He will experience *your* discomfort and in turn may experience it as his own.

Blossom liked to be held in my arms, close to my breasts – the source of her food. She liked to be held by her father in a completely different way. I learnt that Blossom liked to be held quite firmly, and moving around at quite a pace suited her best. Her father always held her in the same way. He allowed Blossom to see her world as he sat her on his arm, holding her firmly for her to scan the wonders of her surroundings. In your explorations with massage, holding and touching, you will be able to discover what is right for your baby.

While some babies like to be held firmly and still, others like to be jiggled gently. Knowing how your baby likes to be held means that others can mirror the holding position and he will be comfortable in their embrace. Spend some time moving around and then keeping still with your baby. Change your holding position and see which position seems to suit him. Watch and observe how others hold your baby and advise them on what suits him.

Before baby Olive reaches the cry stage she will make moaning sounds as if she is about to cry. If someone other than her parents is holding her when she does this, the immediate reaction is to rock or jiggle Olive to soothe her. If you jiggle Olive at this point she becomes tearful and distressed. Knowing that she is simply tired and needs rest means her parents can reassure others that if they stay still and hold her tight she will drop off in no time.

In visiting Sarah and Olive I observed this in action – a beautiful sight for me to see. I observed Sarah placing Olive firmly on her chest, holding her close with both arms wrapped around her. Olive must have felt so wonderfully secure in this embrace as she slept all the while I chatted with her mother.

CHAPTER 4

What is Your Baby Telling You?

Now that you've understood the different aspects of The Blossom Method™ – body language, facial expressions and tongue-talking, you can begin to use these to help your baby in many different ways. Is she hungry? Is she about to fill her nappy? Is she constipated? Is she tired, frustrated or in discomfort? Is she showing the early signs of illness? Read on to find out more and begin to use The Blossom Method™ to really help and understand your baby.

Your Hungry Baby

My research has shown that a great deal of information relating to hunger or thirst is presented by the mouth, lips and, in babies under 12 weeks, by the use of the tongue. In all of the babies I have studied I have found a very similar tongue-talking action. The 'I am hungry or thirsty tongue' can be described in the following way: a soft, rounded tongue placed on the lips that protrudes in and out the baby's mouth. It remains central rather than moving from side to side.

Try this for yourself. Poke your tongue out of your mouth and draw it back into your mouth. Poke it out again and draw it back in. The speed and effort involved in the baby's tongue movement offer further information in relation to the level of hunger. A rapidly moving tongue suggests 'I am very hungry' and a more pedestrian protrusion suggests 'I'm a little hungry or I would like to comfort myself through recreating a sucking action'.

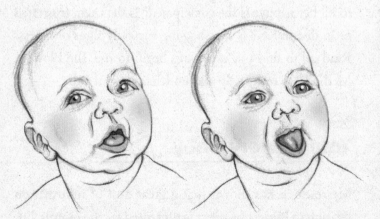

The hungry tongue – moving in and out of the mouth

When Blossom was just a few days old I had already noted her tongue movements as described above. I began to instinctively mirror them back and I became curious as to what this tongue-talking meant to her. I firstly mirrored and then I presented her with my breast for feeding. At this stage I followed my instinct and I was delighted when she latched on. In seeing this tongue-talking again, I simply repeated the actions. In later months I used Blossom's language to enquire about her hunger. I used the tongue-talking that she had presented to me back to her. Would she then mirror it back? Yes, she did. I then took this to mean she was hungry and I was able to ask her if she was hungry, allow her to respond and then feed her.

As well as using their tongue, some babies make an 'O' shape with the mouth open and lips pushed forward. When your baby presents the 'O' shape, again you mirror

The hungry 'O' shape mouth

it back and respond accordingly. When a baby is *very* hungry or thirsty the tongue may protrude further and the 'O' shape may be more pronounced and will be repeated with more speed and effort too. Observe these differences and mirror with the same enthusiasm and speed as your baby before responding as quickly as possible.

> *Baby Georgia presented an 'O' shape and she used her tongue. She seemed to use her lips slightly more than she used her tongue-talking. Her mother and father mirrored both of these back to her. They carefully noted that Georgia appeared to use her lips when trying to secure the breast and her 'O' shape when looking for comfort and contact. I see this as her individual communication.*

We all have different methods of communicating, so the way baby Georgia and other babies communicate will vary too. The Blossom Method™ is here to support you to observe your baby and look out for the suggested tongue-talking and lip patterns, but it also recognises the individuality of your baby and the choices she makes.

> *Interestingly enough I had the pleasure of working with a tongue-tied baby and, although his tongue had limited mobility, he still used his tongue as much as he*

could and had seemingly created a mouth pattern of his own to indicate his hunger. In requesting a feed, he opened his lips and made an 'O' shape. I encouraged his mother to mirror back this communication and respond to him with a feed. I asked her to continue to practise this with him so that he could use his lip and mouth action more to secure his feeds.

So to incorporate The Blossom Method™ in relation to responding to hunger or thirst, you do as always – **observe**, **mirror** and **respond**.

Observe the tongue or mouth pattern in action. You will quickly identify your own baby's style of tongue-talking. Where development and mobility remain unimpaired, it will be similar to the images above.

Mirror the shape and movement. Following your observation, simply mirror the tongue shape, or mouth or lip patterns, with your own tongue or mouth. Whatever shape or pattern is presented, simply copy it and do it back to your baby.

Respond by placing the breast or bottle within reach of your baby's mouth to satisfy her need and reassure her that she has been seen, heard and understood. See what happens next. If your baby is hungry she will latch on, consume her food and be satisfied before she reaches the crying stage. And if your baby is seeking comfort or contact then observe, mirror and respond to this and meet her needs in this way too.

Initially you will find that your own observations and mirroring will encourage return mirroring from your baby. This is a very early form of communication – a system that allows you to demonstrate to one another that you know and understand what is being said. The tongue-talking will become more pronounced when your baby's need increases and when a baby wakes up for a feed. In these instances it's important not to panic in your response. Take time to observe, mirror and respond by offering milk.

In the early stages of my research, I worked with Cat and her baby Sebastian. I met Sebastian and Cat when he was 10 weeks old. He was a lively, curious and interested baby, who appeared to be reaching all of the normal milestones. After hours of observation I was able to conclude he seemed to offer the same 'hungry' tongue-talking shape as Blossom. This was a soft, rounded and flaccid tongue, presented centrally on the lips and which protruded in and out according to his level of hunger. In meeting Sebastian at 10 weeks we introduced him to The Blossom Method™, which was much later than I had used it on my daughter, Blossom. Following such intensive observation, I was interested in why he seemed to use his tongue less than

*Blossom and some of the other babies I had observed.
After much more global research I am now aware that
some babies use their lips and mouths more than their
tongue. Nonetheless he did use the same tongue pattern
as her to indicate hunger. Once we had been able to
discover his hungry tongue-talking, I encouraged Cat
to observe Sebastian's body language, facial expressions
and tongue-talking to see what she felt about his non-
verbal communication. Cat was delighted to discover
the meaning of many of his non-verbal expressions. I
encouraged Cat to mirror his tongue-talking and, in
particular, his hungry tongue-talking. She soon mas-
tered the art of The Blossom Method™. In spotting the
tongue, she mirrored it back. Sebastian mirrored it
back to her and she fed him.*

'I had learnt about The
Blossom Method™ and tongue-
talking before Sam was born so I was
looking for the hungry tongue. Sometimes
it was hard to stop myself from responding
quickly by offering the breast as soon as I saw it,
but I quickly got into the habit of mirroring before responding with the breast. Sam seemed
to know that I'd spotted his hungry tongue
and felt reassured so we never got to the
crying stage with him.' – Gemma and
her 14-week-old baby boy

Searching tongue

One of the first things a mother will notice about her newborn is the way the baby searches for the breast. Babies searching for the breast will snuffle and shuffle as well as offer information with their tongue and eye-gaze. If you stroke your baby's cheek she will turn her head and prepare herself ready for a feed. I believe the tongue and/or mouth are where this rooting reflex begins. The searching tongue can be described as a protruding tongue, a soft shape, protruding in and out of the mouth and moving from side to side. The tongue may come right out of your baby's mouth or the lips will make the 'O' shape as they search out their nourishment. The tongue is placed at each side of the baby's lips and she will stroke the lips with her tongue as she moves it from one side of her mouth to

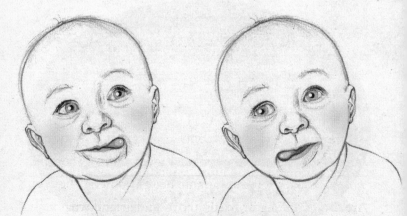

The searching tongue – moving from right to left

the other. Alongside the searching tongue, I have noted eye-scanning in babies too.

I observed Blossom's searching tongue from the day she was born! Her tongue would slide across her lips and as she grew she would scan her domain with enthusiasm. In seeing this tongue and her eye-scanning, I would offer her comfort and physical contact. I also addressed her need to feed and confirmed that her non-verbal communication indicated a search for the breast.

In working with a baby of 10 weeks I noted his eye-scanning immediately. Baby Sebastian's mummy Cat left the room to put the kettle on. This 10-week-old baby scanned his domain and noted the absence of his mother immediately. He then placed his eye-gaze with me. As soon as she returned from the kitchen, his gaze was firmly fixed on his mummy. Following her fleeting absence he sought comfort from her and used his eyes and lip pattern to secure his mother's hold and her breast.

Observe: When you notice this movement, watch carefully to see how the tongue moves, where it touches and what shape it forms. Simultaneously observe the eyes. Are they scanning or fixed? Try to understand what your baby is looking for.

Mirror: Copy your baby's expressions and present the tongue pattern (and eye-gaze when noted) back to her.

Respond: After mirroring back, respond by placing the breast or bottle in reach of your baby's mouth. If she latches on or begins to consume her bottle, then your baby has found what she had been searching for. If she continues to use her tongue, mouth and/or eye-gaze, she probably wishes to simply investigate her surroundings and make contact with you.

Babies use this tongue pattern when they are searching for the breast, and as suggested they also scan with their eyes.

It is important to emphasise that the searching for the breast, or indeed 'milk from a bottle', tongue should be responded to with care. Following your **observations** you can **mirror** back the tongue pattern and simply **respond** to your baby's needs by placing the breast or bottle within reach of the mouth. Do not put the breast or teat directly into your baby's mouth. Encourage your baby to reach for what she wants rather than forcing upon her what you think she might want. Ensure that you are attentive without taking control. Your baby will latch on and will gain confidence from the fact that she had some control over getting her needs and desires met. Here we see the locus of control given to the baby, and we see the simple three-step process in action again – **observe**, **mirror** and

respond. This demonstrates once again baby-led parenting at its best!

> *I recently observed a mother and her 15-week-old daughter. We observed the baby's tongue-talking in action. She initially produced a 'searching' tongue, a protruding tongue gliding across her lips and then a searching for a feed tongue. Her tongue moved in and out of her mouth. It was central to her lips. Her tongue movement appeared to be insistent but not over-anxious. From this I gathered she was hungry or thirsty but not desperate for her feed – just simply hungry and thirsty. The baby's tongue moved in and out of her mouth as if she was searching for something. Her eyes held a piercing gaze that intermittently scanned the area as if in search of something. What was she searching for? The mother proceeded to take out her bottle and feed her baby. As the mother moved towards her baby's bottle and prepared to feed her baby, her baby moved her arms and legs. She seemed excited and happy in her non-verbal utterances. We could all see her baby was indeed thirsty and hungry. The milk was consumed in an instant!*

Another mother I worked with told me that her six-week-old baby produced 'lip-smacking' noises to indicate his hunger. Although this is a verbal clue, I felt it was useful to include this in the section relating to indicators of hunger. I have seen this in other babies too. They moisten their lips and tap the lips together, making a gentle noise. Listen out for this, as it will be an early indicator of hunger.

I have also seen in many babies the excitement of having their needs met in a kicking action. Just before being fed your baby may well kick her legs with joy and excitement. I have noted this in babies over 12 weeks old.

> *Baby Olive was introduced to The Blossom Method™ from birth and was a prolific tongue-talker! Olive used her tongue to indicate which breast she wanted to nourish herself from. She would point it towards the left or right breast, and Blossom also indicated in this way. Olive's mum told me that if she tried to place the other breast in front of Olive she refused to latch on. Her tongue would slide, point and protrude towards the one she wanted.*

Windy Tongue Movement or Facial Expression

Your baby is likely to cry if she has wind, but before she does she will produce non-verbally many expressions that can allow you to understand what she is experiencing.

Observe: She will have a full facial expression – a flaccid yet full-looking bottom lip, with an overall expression of fullness. She may produce a strained expression and may wriggle in discomfort. Following a satisfying feed, babies tend to display a flaccid tongue that may perch loosely on the lower lip. Their lips appear full and their eye-gaze a little dreamy. This flaccid tongue and full bottom lip indicates that a baby is full and needs winding. In observing all of the non-verbal clues provided by your baby, you can quickly respond long before she experiences any possible discomfort.

Mirror: In noting these expressions, simply mirror them back. In your observation note the lips, the cheeks, the general presentation and the eye-gaze. Copy what you see and then show this to your baby. In your observations and subsequent mirroring, she will feel like she has been seen and therefore 'heard'. If your baby produces a strained smile or winces in discomfort, mirror this expression too. The mirroring of these expressions will support your baby to release her wind and discomfort.

Respond: Pat and rub your baby's back or chest or use whichever technique relieves your baby's wind.

The windy tongue

Directional tongue-talking

I can recall in our early non-verbal communication Blossom would not feed from one of my breasts. She would use her tongue to point towards the breast she wanted. No matter how hard I tried to get her to latch on to the other breast she wouldn't. After two to three days of struggling with this, I began to experience pain and soreness in the 'rejected' breast. I had an infection in this breast and I believe that Blossom knew about this days before I did and this is why she chose not to secure her feed from this breast. As soon as the infection cleared she returned to securing her feed from both breasts.

With this directional tongue-talking, I would advise the following: if you have observed the hungry tongue-talking and begun to mirror this, but in response your baby appears to reject your breast, I advise you to offer the other breast to see if this is what she is seeking. Practising The Blossom Method™ will help you both to develop your communication skills. The more you tune in to your baby, the more you will understand.

Reflux

Reflux occurs when the valve between the stomach and oesophagus (windpipe) is weak, resulting in an inability to keep milk down. If your baby is experiencing distress associated with digestion or reflux you should see your doctor or health visitor; however, the information below may be helpful.

Vicki, who is a mother of three, found her youngest baby was showing signs of the reflux. At eight weeks he was crying for hours at a time and was difficult to settle, causing stress in the family and anxiety for Vicki. I spoke to Vicki about this and suggested that she try to make her body language more calm and relaxed to help calm her baby. If we become distressed it is written in our facial expressions and body language, and our babies pick up on this. Non-verbal mirroring can be both positive and negative. Your baby's distress will be distressing to you, but if you display your own non-verbal or indeed verbal signs of distress this can potentially exacerbate a difficult situation.

To treat reflux, the baby should be held upright facing away from you. Do not lay your baby down on a flat surface. If you lay her down, you will notice further discomfort. It is as if she finds it more difficult to find relief from her reflux. If you do want to put her down, raise the area behind her head and upper back slightly. In picking your baby up, avoid jiggling her as this could cause further discomfort and reflux. In your embrace, firmly place your hand on your baby's back and keep her as still as possible. Wind your baby regularly and support your baby to feed for short intervals. Feeding at speed may cause further distress and discomfort. You may also want to swaddle her in a soft sheet. This will help her to feel contained. This containing feeling is a repetition of the time she was held in the womb, swaddled inside of you.

Colic

Colic is when a healthy baby has bouts of uncontrollable crying. It is believed to occur in around a fifth of babies from when they are 2–3 weeks old and it usually lasts until they are 3–4 months old. It can be very challenging and difficult for parents because the baby will be inconsolable. As well as crying, a colicky baby may pull her legs up to her tummy, and also arch her back and pass wind when crying. If your baby is experiencing distress associated with colic, speak to your doctor or health visitor, but also see the advice below.

Theories on colic appear to vary, but many people consider colic to be associated with tension and rigidity and tautness in the digestive system. It may also be associated with anxiety. As with reflux (see above), colic needs to be managed well. It is likely that you will feel anxious and distressed if your baby is experiencing colic, but try not to show how upset you are as this will add to your baby's distress. If you become tearful and anxious and you flood your system with stress hormones, your baby will pick up on your distress. This will increase the feelings of anxiety in your baby. If you do become distressed, please try to take a minute or two to compose yourself. Think of what is best for your baby and how best you can support her in her discomfort. In using The Blossom Method™ you will be able to demonstrate you have noted your baby's distress through observation and non-verbal mirroring. In colic your baby's legs may be drawn upwards. If you are seated you could draw your legs upwards too. This is not the most important part of mirroring this experience. The most important element is to mirror the discomfort of your baby and then quickly respond to her by holding or swaddling her through this. Swaddling is comforting to

'My baby, Lois, was fine for the first month or so, then she developed colic. We had no idea what it was or why she developed it. We visited our GP who told us it was colic. In the evening she would cry for hours and this was so distressing for all of us. I felt it was important to keep my distress to a minimum as I knew this would only make us all feel worse.' – Elizabeth and her five-month-old baby girl

most babies as it recreates that sense of being held in the
womb. Be guided by your baby's response. If her tears and
distress dissipate, then you know your actions are working
well. If her tears and distress become more pronounced,
then simply try an alternative response and move your
'holding' position to suit your little one. This will require
a little bit of trial and error. Once you have succeeded in
knowing how to soothe your baby through colic, retain
the information and use this again as the need arises.

Your Toileting Baby

A baby may find some fear or discomfort in the actual
experience of moving her bowels or urinating. If she does,
she may begin to whimper or indeed cry while doing so. If
she is damp or can feel the full nappy against her skin, she
may become distressed. My research has shown specific
tongue, lip or mouth movements occur in babies prior to
urinating and having a bowel movement. If you are available to use The Blossom Method™, then your baby can
go through this experience without reaching the crying
stage. I have also noted particular expressions and tongue
patterns in babies experiencing constipation. Babies
appear to provide us with the same non-verbal signs but
then fail to have a bowel movement. If you are able to

identify your baby's tongue-talking in relation to constipation, you can help her to relieve it before she becomes too distressed. In addition to responding non-verbally, you can add verbal expressions to your utterances – mirroring your baby's verbal expressions as you help her make sense of her world.

When she had bowel movements, Blossom used to offer a pointed, protruding tongue that would be pushed out as far as she could, minutes and sometimes seconds before she filled her nappy. I would simply mirror back this tongue (to show her I had 'heard' her) and then prepare myself and her for a nappy change or an investigation of her level of comfort after she had filled her nappy. She also expressed herself in the very same way with constipation; her body and facial expressions would be the same, but she would be unable to move her bowels. In noting the expressions (**observation**) and realising nappy-filling hadn't occurred I would **mirror** her expression and **respond** by offering her more breast milk and/or water to eliminate her discomfort and support her to move her bowels. I was delighted to recognise her poo-tongue – others seemed surprised by my insight!

I must confess to using my knowledge and insight of Blossom's 'poo' tongue with both humour and confidence. Sometimes, on noting Blossom's poo tongue, I confidently handed her to my husband or other unsuspecting family member to allow them to manage the 'poo' situation for themselves!

Poo and wee tongue

A baby's facial expressions are often particularly expressive when she needs to urinate or have a bowel movement. Young babies are said to urinate on average every 20–25 minutes. On average they move their bowels between 20–30 minutes after each feed and they are inclined to move their bowels after having a sleep.

Look for signs such as taut lips, a strained smile, wincing, a protruding and/or pointed tongue, a look of distress or discomfort, an arched back and a taut tummy. Look for consistent tongue and mouth shapes that are presented just prior to a particular action or request from your baby (tongue patterns are seen from a few seconds up to a few minutes before). The tongue patterns are repeated; this will give you plenty of opportunity to observe. The majority of babies I have studied present the tongue repeatedly as a pointed and almost sharp-looking shape, which extends fully both prior to urinating and prior to any bowel movements. Some of the babies I have observed have used their mouth and lips more than their tongues and they have presented me with taut lips or a strained smile as well as a look of discomfort and distress. Look at your baby's eyes too. In moving her bowels, she may have a puzzled look in her eyes. I have seen this in babies who are less than 12 weeks old. As the moving bowels and urinating tongue patterns or shapes look very similar, pay close attention. The tip of the tongue is usually pointed and tends to poke out of the mouth and remain there for a few seconds before being drawn back in. As always, this is repeated.

There may be variations – for example, when urinating your baby may demonstrate a slight curl to the edges of each side of the tongue. Additional information will be found in your baby's body language. Some babies may simply use the 'O' shape for their version of poo or wee tongue-talking. Some may use their tongue-talking briefly but the most dominant expression may simply be a strained smile.

The poo and wee tongue

In one of my early meetings with Sarah, mother to Olive, I had suggested that Sarah look for the most obvious of non-verbal expressions, which is that relating to bowel movement. It is useful to start with what is obvious as this helps you to build your confidence in working with the non-verbal. They soon picked up on Olive's strained smile. Sarah told me, 'When Olive was just two weeks old we knew she was struggling to do a poo. We learnt her poo face very early on as it's very expressive! One of her many pooing facial expressions is a strained smile. My husband held Olive so she could see his face clearly. Each time Olive repeated her strained smile expression, we imitated and mirrored the strained smile back to her. Olive then mirrored it back again. After a few repetitions we could hear quite clearly that things were moving down there!' Sarah and Peter felt both excited and pleased that they had managed to have a greater understanding of their baby Olive. This excitement and happiness was apparent and could also be seen, felt and experienced by baby Olive, both non-verbally and verbally.

I have noted joyful expressions in many babies whose parents use The Blossom Method™. I believe that this sort of early communication goes a long way to relieving the anxiety of new parents. I believe that understanding one another to this degree will maximise contentment and minimise worry.

Observe: Learn to identify your baby's tongue movements and expressions in relation to urinating and bowel movements.

Mirror: Simply copy the tongue-talking and mirror it back with the same amount of enthusiasm.

Respond: You can then respond by managing your baby's nappy-filling activities with as little anxiety as possible. Think about your facial expressions here too. Keep upbeat and positive. If your baby is distressed, you can mirror back her expression ('I have seen and heard you') and then smile in order to help her feel more at ease.

TIP

Your baby will urinate on average every 25 minutes, so don't feel that you have to change her nappy every time she has had a wee. Think about the environment, the cost and landfill! Your baby will be fine for a little while.

Jen was amazed when I showed her how to recognise baby Ciara's toileting tongue. She soon learnt the facial expressions and mouth and tongue patterns that meant Ciara was toileting and was able to deal with

her nappy quickly and easily before Ciara experienced
any discomfort or began to whimper. She found that
Ciara was happy and more contented, something she
mirrored back to Jen.

Constipation

Observe: Interestingly, the tongue-talking and expressions outlined above for bowel movements are produced even if a baby is constipated, which can be useful when trying to understand why she may be uncomfortable or agitated. In observing your baby, you will begin to notice her mouth, lips or tongue patterns. You may also notice straining expressions or other facial expressions that will allow you to elicit more information. Look out for signs of discomfort, such as a tension in the stomach area, wriggling in discomfort, raising her knees to her chest or an arching of the back. These will be further clues as to the level of comfort or potential discomfort.

Mirror: Mirror back the expressions as seen. Pay close attention as your baby will provide these expressions quickly. Do not worry if you seem to be missing them – the more you observe your baby, the more you will see. The more you see, the more you can mirror.

Respond: If you spot these tongue movements and expressions and a soiled nappy doesn't follow, you could offer the breast, bottle or cooled boiled water to see if any of these help move the bowels.

In observing Blossom as a baby, I would note the presence of her poo tongue when she hadn't moved her bowels. This happened occasionally. She would present us with a taut tummy, an arched back and she would wriggle in her distress. She would move her head from side to side and frown in her frustration. This non-verbal communication combination allowed us to understand Blossom's needs and respond accordingly, thereby reducing her distress.

In observing baby Sebastian, I noted that his non-verbal cues and clues for constipation were similar to those of other babies. I observed, as did his mother, Cat, that when Sebastian was constipated he would kick his legs and wriggle in his discomfort. She also noted he would tighten his tummy and, finally, before he reached the crying stage he would arch his back. Once Cat noted his non-verbal expressions for constipation, she could manage this better. Firstly, she would understand for herself what the problem was, secondly, she could show Sebastian that she knew what the problem was, and, thirdly, she could support Sebastian with his constipation by offering him breast milk or water to support him to relieve himself.

Potty training

As your baby grows, you may want to use your knowledge and insight into your baby's toileting habits to aid you in potty training. In observing the urinating or bowel-movement tongue shape, you can take your baby to a potty or a toilet and encourage her to use this instead of nappies. As you will develop a deeper understanding of your baby's non-verbal expressions through practising The Blossom Method™, you will be familiar with her particular signs and signals and, as a result, this will help you to implement early potty training. Have your potty handy and simply look out for all of the expressions you've noted to date. When you see your baby's tongue-talking or strained smile, etc., remove her nappy and mirror back her expressions, then quickly place the potty underneath her. Potty training is seen as important to the emotional bond between a baby and carer. It also promotes further the need for parents to pick up on subtle body language expressions and tongue/mouth patterns that, if responded to, will promote a successful transition towards potty training.

Discomfort, Tiredness and Frustration

Your baby will sometimes experience discomfort, tiredness and frustration. She may be finding it difficult to latch on and secure a feed. She may be tired and unable to sleep. She may be experiencing pain through constipation. She may be feeling unwell, with a fever. If you are sure that her distress, tiredness and frustration are manageable and you have no concerns in relation to her health and wellbeing, then I would advise you to look out for other non-verbal messages to see if these will deepen your understanding of your baby.

The verbal and non-verbal messages need to be clear.

1. Your baby needs to know she has been 'seen' and therefore heard in her distress (**observation**).
2. She needs to know through non-verbal and verbal mirroring that you understand her pain, distress and discomfort (**mirroring**).
3. Your baby needs to feel contained in her discomfort (**response**).

Here we see how The Blossom Method™ can be used to great effect. Babies need to feel that they can be loved, cared for and emotionally 'held'. They do not want to feel that you are unable to contain their discomfort, pain or distress. Positive care and effective containing will be experienced and felt by your baby as you develop your skills in managing her discomfort or frustration, and as you display to her, non-verbally and verbally, your ability to understand her experience and remain present. In 'containing' we are seeking to be able to manage efficiently our baby's experiences. You are 'containing' the experience without bringing your own feelings about it into play.

Arched back and a taut tummy

Observe: Babies tend to arch their backs, push their stomachs forward, raise their knees upwards towards their chests and wriggle when experiencing discomfort. Your baby's facial expression may be one of obvious distress. If you see a strained, sad-looking face, look beyond this and see what other non-verbal cues can be seen. Do her eyes look full of sparkle or are they flat and dull looking? Is she presenting you with a strained expression? I have noted side-to-side head movements in babies experiencing discomfort. Does your baby move her head as if she is saying no?

Mirror: Use your knowledge and observations to focus upon the facial expressions of discomfort. Mirror these facial and head movement expressions back ('I have seen and heard you'). Understandably, it may be a little more difficult to mirror your baby's whole body expression, especially if you are in the middle of your weekly shop!

Respond: Your baby needs to know she has been seen and heard. This will come from both your observation and your response. In seeing these displays of discomfort, respond by holding your baby in order to observe closely her expressions. Then look for signs of hunger (the hungry tongue-talking – see page 73) or to see if she is constipated (see page 96). Depending on what you find, you can then meet your baby's needs.

Kicking legs

Observe: A baby might kick her legs for two reasons. Firstly she may kick her legs in excitement, exactly as observed in a baby securing a feed. Alternatively, a baby may kick her legs in frustration or discomfort. If your baby is kicking and this seems to be linked to frustration rather than excitement, this is a useful sign to pick up on. It could indicate pain, constipation or a desire to be heard and held. You will quickly learn the difference between excitement and frustration. If you are able to spend time on the observation part of The Blossom Method™, you will see the difference between what can be loosely described as positive and negative non-verbal expressions. Just as we are able to note and experience the differences between a happy face and a sad face, look out for your baby shaking her head as if she is saying no. Look out for a frown or a furrowed brow. And look out too for eyes that appear to be smiling. You can certainly present smiling eyes without having a smile on your lips.

Mirror: If you are seated, then following your observation you can mirror the kicking too. I did this with Blossom, and it felt like I was saying to her, 'I can see and hear you, I know what you are experiencing.' Blossom was initially curious. She would briefly slow down while I mirrored her, then as I slowed my kicking down she would speed hers up. She was joyful in our mirroring. She loved it. Baby Sebastian responded in a similar way to Blossom. He kicked his legs in both excitement and frustration. He slowed his kicking down as he observed with interest my kicking and then he would speed up again. It was as if he was trying to discover if he was in charge of the kicking legs he could see before him. Both his and mine.

Respond: If your baby is excited, she may be looking for a feed or looking to be held, or she may simply be excited to see you. You will soon be able to distinguish between the types of excitement and will know which type of response to offer. If your baby is distressed, try to respond by initially mirroring and looking at your baby's body language, facial expression and body movement. If she is kicking her legs and shuffling, look in her nappy. If she is arching her back and presenting you with a taut tummy and kicking her legs, this may be a sign of wind. If her legs are raised up towards the tummy and she is distressed, this could be a further sign of wind and constipation. Respond by using wind-relief techniques, such as patting and rubbing. In the case of constipation, breastfeed or give your baby water to drink.

Fist clenching

Observe: If your baby is tired, she may clench her fists – as if poised to fight away the first signs of tiredness. Clenched fists can also be a sign of distress or frustration. What is your baby experiencing when she clenches her fists? What does this baby body language mean to you and your baby? Is she tired or is she communicating a different need?

'When Poppy is frustrated she waves her fists in the air. Her hands reach up and she grabs the air. I know she's frustrated when she does this.'
– Joanna and her seven-week-old baby girl

Mirror: I enjoyed mirroring Blossom's arm and hand movements too. You can do the same if you so wish. Once again mirror the arm movements with as much enthusiasm as is being presented by your baby. I have seen a slowing down of arm movements in babies who are being mirrored. As your baby observes your mirroring, see if you have noted a look of curiosity and a slowing down of arm movements. If you feel less inclined to mirror these movements, simply observe your baby's facial expressions, eye-gaze and mood and mirror these non-verbal expressions back. I am aware some of you may feel more self-conscious than others. Just do what feels right for you.

Respond: Your response here will be dependent upon your findings. If your baby is frustrated, show her that you have seen, heard and understood her by presenting her with her non-verbal expressions. If your baby is frustrated, help her to feel less frustrated by trying to understand

TIP

If your baby appears to be experiencing a significant sense of frustration, make sure she is feeding well. I have noted frustration in tongue-tied babies who have not been able to latch on properly. If you are concerned about this, ask your health visitor, doctor or other healthcare professional to check your baby's tongue for tongue-tie. In this condition, the string of tissue (frenulum) that attaches the tongue to the floor of the mouth is too short, preventing the tongue from moving freely.

what it is she requires to ease her frustration. Is she simply bored? Does she require a change of scenery? If so, it is simple enough to move her. Does she require comfort and your contact? If so, she may need you to

'Following my newfound interest in baby body language I note when Olive is tired; she waves her clenched fists in the air.' – Sarah and her five-week-old baby girl

hold her for a while. If she is under-stimulated, provide some additional stimuli for her. If you are busy then provide an age-appropriate toy, such as a hanging mobile, for her to observe. Is she frustrated through constipation? If so, look out for additional tongue-talking and mouth or lip patterns (see page 96) to see if this is the case.

In my research I've found that individual babies use similar non-verbal arm and fist movements, but that the meaning of the movement for each baby can be quite different. While one baby might wave her arms and fists in the air in frustration, others might express discomfort with the arms and clenched fists. Blossom's arm and fist movement tended to relate to her tiredness.

Observing tiredness

Not all of your observations can be mirrored. The following body language observations may help you develop a deeper understanding of what your baby is experiencing. Observe carefully and respond to these observations and you will continue to develop and deepen your communication with your baby.

When a baby is tired, there is sometimes a change in the skin tone beneath the eyebrows. In a baby with dark skin, the skin around the eyes and particularly under the eyebrows will become darker. In a pale-skinned tired baby, the skin beneath the eyebrows may become pink, and as tiredness increases, if the baby is unable to sleep, it may darken in colour to become almost red. Being aware

'The areas around Sebastian's eyebrows turn red when he is hungry. I have noticed this since we have discussed baby body language signs. Even though I had seen this change, I had no idea I could work out what this meant. I became really curious and wondered, what does this mean to him? When I worked it out I was really pleased I knew. I am now able to meet his needs and feed him before he reaches the crying stage.' – Cat and her 10-week-old baby boy

'Oh, he so does the red eyebrow thing! We call these his tired eyebrows.' – Paula and her 12-week-old baby boy

of the skin tone of your baby in this area will help you read the signs that may also be indicated in other expressions and movements.

An obvious expression relates to drooping eyelids just before falling asleep. All of us have probably seen this in our babies and other family members across the generations! Often the baby, following a satisfying feed, will begin to display drooping eyelids. In doing so she is indicating satisfaction and a readiness to sleep.

I have observed this in many of the babies I've worked with. Blossom enjoyed breastfeeding and, as such, she latched on and fed herself until she was satisfied. I noticed her drooping eyelids on numerous occasions. I instinctively mirrored her drooping eyelids and was able to either continue holding her or place her down in her bed to rest.

As my mum held her newborn granddaughter, she noticed (from an instinctive level) that Blossom's body felt warmer. My mum suggested that Blossom was about to fall asleep. I asked her how she knew she was about to drop off, and her response

'One of the first things I noticed about Rosie's eyes and eyebrows was the skin colour changes. Her skin changes colour around her eyes and underneath her eyebrows to pink and red.' – Helen and her five-week-old baby girl

was: 'She's gone all warm now.' My mum said that she experienced this with me as a baby as well. I thought this observation was so simple, but also so incredible.

In my research, I have been fortunate to hold many babies in my arms. In all the babies who have slept in my arms, I have noticed an increase in body warmth just prior to sleeping.

Recognising Signs of Illness

If you have concerns about your baby's health and well-being, then always use a thermometer to check your baby's temperature accurately and seek medical assistance when you feel it is required. What makes you decide to check the temperature of your baby? Is it the verbal utterances, such as crying, or is it what you see and feel? What information are you attuning to first? You might gather information regarding body temperature by looking, feeling and hearing.

Observation and understanding of what has been seen can indicate how a baby is feeling. It can also help parents predict when their child is about to fall ill. Parents have repeatedly reported to me that the smell of their children's breath changes when they fall ill. The odour is slightly different for each child but may have a glue-like scent and usually appears 24–36 hours before the onset of the illness. This sign remains throughout childhood so this can be a useful check to perform whenever you notice that something's not quite right or that your child appears under the weather or reluctant to participate in activities.

If Blossom appears 'not quite herself' or 'under the weather', the first thing I do is, instinctively, to smell her breath. If it has a glue-like quality, we are in no doubt that she is 'coming down with something'. The glue smell is almost identical to the kind of glue I was allowed to use in craft-making in my teens. It has a strong and powerful odour and one I cannot forget. It is only ever present when Blossom is ill. This 'tell' is very powerful. One weekend Blossom fell ill. She had viral symptoms such as vomiting and so on. She appeared to be particularly unwell. Blossom is an articulate person and as such she could clearly tell us her symptoms. As a result, I placed my foolproof method of smelling her breath on hold. We were advised to take Blossom to the out-of-hours doctor at our local hospital. Upon arrival I sat down and then instinctively observed Blossom's skin tone, her body posture, her voice tone, her breathing, her eye-gaze and the 'glue-like' smell on her breath. I immediately knew Blossom was really quite unwell. Her skin tone had a yellowish tinge. Her shoulders were slumped in her lack of energy and discomfort. Her voice lacked energy and enthusiasm. Her breathing was noticeably slow and shallow.

A new mum emailed me and said her newborn was tearful and generally 'out of sorts'. I asked her to smell his breath to see if she noted any differences. She said his breath didn't smell normal. In asking what his normal breath smell was like, she described it as sweet and milky. After smelling his breath she went on to say: 'His breath smells funny,' and I explained that this was likely to be a sign that he was unwell. After about 24 hours she noticed further signs of ill health – a cold-type illness. The mother said she felt prepared for the fact that he might become unwell and as a result was less worried about him being less happy than normal. By minimising her anxiety, she was better able to care for her unwell baby. Again, I believe that this was the ill-health breath smell noted in some babies.

> 'I always knew when Jack was ill. He had a different smell about him.' – Karen and her seven-week-old baby boy

Take a moment to familiarise yourself with your baby's breath smell.

A fever

If your baby has a fever, then her body will overheat and she may become distressed and uncomfortable. Look out for all the possible non-verbal clues such as changes in skin tone and increased heat. Is your baby red in the cheeks and hot to touch? Fever could be a possible sign of infection. Always have a thermometer at home and check her temperature. It is considered normal for a baby to have a body temperature of about 36–37° Celsius (96.8–98.6° Fahrenheit). You should be aware of these figures prior to assessing your baby's temperature. We need to be aware that a slight change in temperature may be a sign of ill health and we must consider contacting the doctor immediately. Babies can become severely ill very quickly, so if your baby exhibits any symptoms in addition to the fever, such as breathing problems, listlessness, vomiting or diarrhoea, take her to see a doctor immediately. As a capable, caring and loving parent you should decide when medical intervention is necessary. If you feel it is, then don't hesitate to seek medical advice.

When Blossom had a fever and became unwell she was generally 'not herself'. She would be restless, irritable and tearful. She would shake her head from side to side as if she was saying no. Her skin tone was different – she was pale but red in the cheeks – and she was listless. Her breath had a glue-like odour, different from usual. Her eyes looked less lively.

Responding to accidents

It is realistic enough to think that your baby will cry if she hurts herself. However, how does a baby know to what degree she has hurt herself? How does she know if she is badly or only slightly hurt? Much of this information will be transferred non-verbally and verbally from you to your baby and from your baby to you. She will respond to your actions or responses, both verbal and non-verbal.

Many parents have placed their baby on a couch, bed or other surface and to their horror the baby has rolled off. It's such a shocking experience for you both. Often, up until this point, their baby has been unable to roll over; it's a skill she has developed and is experimenting with. This is an occasion where you may not be able to meet the needs of your baby before she cries, but what you can do is minimise your own and your baby's distress by responding as quickly as possible and by keeping as calm as you can.

The following experience I had with Blossom is, unfortunately, seemingly shared by many others. I had placed Blossom on our bed and up until this point she had been unable to roll over. As I went to gather a clean nappy and a sleepsuit, she rolled off the bed. Although I felt horrified, anxious and distressed I instantly picked Blossom up and held her close. I tried to minimise both my verbal and non-verbal expression to help minimise hers. I quickly became aware that her expression was initially fairly neutral but seemingly startled. My facial expression was one of horror. She looked at me and *then* began to cry. I quickly became aware of my non-verbal expression and in an attempt to minimise our distress I soothed her by stroking her face, holding her close and trying to neutralise my expression. This seemed to resolve matters relatively quickly.

Can you see how you can use the concept of The Blossom Method™ here too? Following her fall, I immediately observed Blossom (noting her startled and then neutral facial expression), but I did not right away mirror this as I was too horrified to do so. I responded quickly, though, by holding her close and soothing her. Blossom had then mirrored my negative expression and I initially mirrored this back to her, but quickly changed it to a more neutral one. This soothed us both as quickly as it could. My heartbeat will have been experienced as faster and stress hormones will have been released through the experience of the fall. She will no doubt have a body-held memory associated with this experience.

I work in this way with all injuries, falls, illnesses and so on. I am fully responsive (observe) and I mirror the feelings of any distressed child or baby. The non-verbal (and verbal) messages from the parent to the baby should be, 'You're going to be okay. We can manage this experience. I am sorry you are in distress. Things will be better soon. I am not angry. I love you.' Sometimes our distress, anxiety or anger can make our babies and children feel we are angry with them. This is not a positive message. In minimising *your* anxiety, less of this will be mirrored or projected on to your baby or child.

In this chapter you will have developed your understanding of The Blossom Method™. You will now be able to consider how your **observations**, **mirroring-back** and **responses** have deepened your knowledge of your baby's communication. You will have experienced the joys of baby-led communication and parenting. I think this is wonderful. Expanding your understanding is so empowering for you. It is also a great source of comfort to know you understand what your baby is saying and experiencing. I wonder if you are able to reflect on your journey so far and consider how much more you have learnt through your experience of using The Blossom Method™? More importantly, I wonder how much wellbeing your baby and you have experienced as a result?

CHAPTER 5

The Blossom Method™ and Baby Signing

I hope you have enjoyed using The Blossom Method™ with your baby and that your experience of parenting, as well as your baby's development, has been enhanced by its many benefits. If you'd like to continue with non-verbal methods of communication with your older baby, then baby signing is a good way to do so.

What is Baby Signing?

At its simplest level, think of a baby waving goodbye or raising his arms when he wants to be picked up. These are baby signs we're all familiar with. Your baby understands what he wants and is able to communicate non-verbally long before he can speak. He will naturally use baby signs to express his needs. Child development expert Dr Joseph Garcia studied hearing babies of deaf parents and found that they easily copied their deaf parents' signs in order to communicate. Incredibly, he found that these babies seemed less demanding than non-signing babies because they could so easily express their needs and, as a result, get their needs met. It was through this research that he developed baby signing that could be used by hearing parents of hearing babies.

"I loved using The Blossom Method™ with my baby. It was fun, helpful and it really worked for us. We are now ready to go on to learn baby signing and I can't wait.'
– Danielle and her 20-week-old baby boy

Baby signing is used in conjunction with normal speech, so it does not replace language. In fact, advocates of baby signing believe it can enhance language development. It is believed to support communication, encourage brain activity and enhance a baby's development.

As baby signing expert Deirdre McLaughlin, who teaches baby signing through Sign2Music and is a family practitioner, points out, 'Babies can understand language at a very young age but are unable to communicate this verbally as the muscles needed to use spoken language are not yet developed. Signing with your baby allows them to communicate their wants, needs and observations with you at a much earlier age than if they had been unable to sign. For babies, the ability to understand and make yourself understood fosters self-esteem. In our classes we love to see the delighted little faces when little ones first begin to sign and realise others know what they are trying to tell them. This also deepens their connection with others.'

Your baby is said to be capable of learning signs from the age of six months. I believe he can start much sooner than this. Indeed I have seen it with my very own eyes with a number of babies! You can start at any time and it will not be detrimental for him or you to start before six months. If you use baby signing with consistency, your baby will recognise and understand these signs and may begin to use them much earlier.

The signs in baby signing are taken from sign language but sometimes simplified. Common signs are for words like 'milk', 'food', 'more', 'drink', 'bed', 'mummy' and 'daddy'. As an example, the baby sign for 'milk' requires you to clench your fist and to pulsate the fingers gently as if you are squeezing something – like you are milking an imaginary cow's udder! See the illustrations on pages 119–22 for a range of baby signs.

Most parents normally teach baby signing through attendance at weekly classes. Just like The Blossom Method™, the more you use baby signing the more it will be used, developed and responded to. With regular, daily use baby signing can be learnt well and your baby's skills (and yours) can be developed quickly. Use of a few signs will prove to be a key factor for success.

Some basic baby signs

Here are some simple signs to help you get started with baby signing, courtesy of Cath Smith, author of the LET'S SIGN Series (© 2012 Cath Smith – BSL sign graphics – the LET'S SIGN Series – www.DeafBooks. co.uk). Please see page 136 for resources and places where you can learn further signs.

Please note that these signs are given as if you are right-handed, but if you are left-handed you can use your left hand instead.

You should use your voice to say the words you are signing, such as 'milk' or 'food', to help your baby connect the word in sound, hand movement and lip pattern. Never cover your mouth when you sign, so your baby can clearly see your mouth movements. It is best to also use facial expression and body language with the hand movements to add further meaning to the signs.

Milk

Squeeze your hand into a fist, as if you were 'milking' a cow. Say the word 'milk'.

Food (or eat)

Put your fingertips together and raise your hand towards your mouth as if you were going to eat something. Say the word 'food'.

More

Place your right hand in front of the left hand, then move your hand backwards to tap twice against the left. Say the word 'more'.

Drink

Shape your hand in a 'C' shape, as if holding a cup, then raise and tip it towards your mouth, as if sipping a drink. Say the word 'drink'.

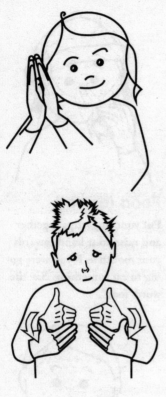

Bed

Place the palms of your hands together by the side of your head. Say the word 'bed'.

Tired

Raise your hands with your thumbs up and your fingertips on your chest. Next, twist your hands down from the wrists so you can see your palms. Say the word 'tired'.

Sleep

Put your index fingers and thumbs out at the sides of your eyes, then pinch your fingers and thumbs together while moving them in front of your eyes. Say the word 'sleep'.

Thank you

With your palm towards you, raise your right hand to your chin, then bring it back down while clearly saying 'thank you'.

Please

As with 'thank you', raise your open right hand towards your chin, then back down again while clearly saying 'please'.

N.B. The signs for 'please' and 'thank you' are the same but the lip patterns are different, so make sure you use a clear lip pattern.

Mummy

Open the palm of your left hand and then tap once with the first three fingers of your right hand on the palm of your left hand. Clearly say 'Mummy'.

Daddy

Take the first two fingers of each hand and tap twice with the right hand's two fingers on top of the left hand's fingers. Clearly say 'Daddy'.

Cold

Squeeze your hands into fists with your elbows close the body and arms. Then shake the fists slightly from side to side, while saying the word 'cold'.

Hot

Place you right hand close to your mouth with your fingers slightly spread out. Then move your hand to the right side, saying the word 'hot'. Ensure your expression conveys a 'warning' component to help your baby associate the danger of hot surfaces.

The Benefits of Baby Signing

Baby signing allows your baby to tell you what he is thinking before he is able to vocalise this with words. He will also be able to tell you that he is hungry, thirsty or tired, or, perhaps, just to tell you he has a wet nappy and would like to have a clean one or even what he would like to play with next. Baby signing supports you and your baby to encapsulate fleeting moments in your child's development. If you use The Blossom Method™ and baby signing you'll capture so much more than if you simply waited for him to develop his speech. Baby signing expert Deirdre McLaughlin says, 'Signing reduces frustration and allows babies to communicate their wants, needs and observations. The ability to communicate also enhances your child's self-esteem.'

Like The Blossom Method™, baby signing can:

- Aid communication between you and your baby.
- Support your baby to continue to feel understood.
- Further support you to understand what your baby needs and wants.
- Reduce frustration in both your baby and you.
- Promote positive brain activity and brain development.
- Reduce the need for your baby to cry.

- Allow you to continue to use gestural language in support of language development.
- Aid speech development and not hinder it.

'Elizabeth started signing back when she was 9 ½ months old, and now, at 12 months, she has nearly 30 signs she uses on a regular basis. It's brilliant, because, instead of getting cross and crying when she wants something, she can tell us exactly what the problem is – whether she's hungry, needs a nappy change, or even if she has seen lights that remind her of stars! I would highly recommend signing classes to anyone with a baby. It's given our daughter a great start in life and us a wonderful gift – the ability to know and share in what she is thinking.' – Anna, mother of two

The Myths about Baby Signing

Many people who are unfamiliar with the world of baby signing have fears and anxieties associated with speech and language delay. I believe that baby signing (and indeed The Blossom Method™) will not only enhance communication but it will also support brain activity and development, which will go on to support the advancement of language and speech. I have met with and spoken to both professionals in the field of baby signing and parents who have given their children the opportunity to learn baby signing, and all the comments and feedback have been positive.

Baby signing expert Louise Gibbs, owner/teacher of the Baby Signing Mummy Method, says, 'I think the most common question I have from parents through my classes is whether or not the Baby Signing Mummy Method will hinder speech in their child. I love being able to answer this misconception as I am able to use examples of all the babies I have taught. As we are always saying the word while making the simple gesture, the baby or toddler is learning the association between the word and the sign and therefore learns the word each time they hear it. This communication is the most important factor in using baby sign

Reading

One of the best things a parent can do with a child is read with them. Signing while reading helps maintain concentration as it engages and involves the child more fully and enables it to be a two-way experience from very early on, helping to foster a love of books while increasing vocabulary and fuelling little imaginations!

language: by repetitively using the word and sign the child will mimic both and often start to say words at a slightly earlier age. For example, I wanted my own daughter to use the phrase "Thank you" instead of the commonly used term "Ta", so each time I signed and said "Thank you" she learnt the phrase and sign. When she was 14 months old she was saying "Thank you" very clearly. She never used the word "Ta" as she didn't know it existed.'

Baby signing expert Deirdre McLaughlin says, 'Many people worry that signing may delay speech development. Research has in fact shown that signing enhances speech development. At Sign2Music we reinforce the spoken word as well as the sign, using signs primarily to facilitate speech development (unless your child has communication difficulties, which affect the ability to communicate verbally). My personal experience and that of many carers who have attended our classes is that signing babies become chatter tots!'

The Transition from The Blossom Method™

I believe using The Blossom Method™ will help you to make the transition to baby signing much earlier. All that is required are your keen observational skills, your mirroring attributes, the consistent use of your baby's Blossom Method™ expressions and an introduction to some of the baby signing signs. It is repetitive use that will promote active participation.

In babies who have been introduced to The Blossom Method™ I have noted a smooth transition between The Blossom Method™ and baby signing at 15 weeks and onwards.

If you have been using The Blossom Method™ with your baby and through doing so you have developed a 'core' list of your baby's non-verbal cues and clues, from 12 weeks onwards you may introduce baby signing in conjunction with The Blossom Method™.

'Azad's first sign was "more". When we played jiggling games he wanted more of that. Then he wanted more and more! I was tired but happy. I then asked if he wanted milk and signed "milk". He was so excited. He could now ask for more milk too!'
– Heather, mother to four

The following case study shows baby Joe using baby signing at 15 weeks. This is because, after using The Blossom Method™, his mother Vicki introduced him to baby signing at 12 weeks and he developed a memory of some signs (such as 'milk', 'more' and 'tired') and he was able to recognise, form and recreate the shapes of the signs his mum used. Vicki told me they consistently used baby signing. It wasn't something they used intermittently.

> In a recent follow-up session with Vicki and her baby
> Joe we spoke more of their journey. I was fortunate to
> observe the ease with which he was able to communicate
> with his mother successfully at just 18 weeks old. Vicki,
> using Joe's mouth movement (learnt by Vicki from Joe
> and discovered through using The Blossom Method™),
> asked Joe if he wanted to feed. He responded by provid-
> ing her with the mouth movement he had produced in
> early infancy and with consistency. His mouth move-
> ment is an 'O' shape. Through observation, mirroring
> back and responding, they had begun to learn that this
> mouth movement was his way of saying he wanted
> a feed. Remember Joe initially showed Vicki his 'O'
> shaped mouth. Vicki quickly learnt to mirror this back
> to him and responded by offering him a feed. They had
> learnt to develop this following our first meeting.
>
> A little later, using The Blossom Method™, she asked
> again if he wanted a feed and this time he did not
> provide her with the mouth pattern to indicate an
> affirmative response so she knew he did not want feed-
> ing. Joe had taught his mum his mouth pattern for
> hunger and she was then able to enquire about his
> hunger during our time together. Towards the end of
> our meeting, she showed me that in addition to using

her voice and The Blossom Method™ mouth movement observations, she had also begun to use the baby sign for milk (see page 119).

At 18 weeks old Joe was able to use both the mouth movement and the baby sign consecutively. The transition from The Blossom Method™ to baby signing was very smooth and seemingly very early.

Vicki and Joe seemed to be successfully making the transition from The Blossom Method™ to baby signing much earlier than most. They have amazing communication. In leaving them I waved at Joe and said goodbye. Joe smiled and waved back at me. I left it for a further 30 seconds and then I repeated the exercise. I waved at Joe and said goodbye. Joe waved goodbye to me. He instantly and successfully mirrored my movement with such ease. Joe seemed to know that we were leaving and he seemed to be very happy in both the fact that he knew what was going on and that he had been understood well during our two-hour meeting.

Hands-on Signing

'Hands-on' signing is the language of the deaf-blind community. It takes many of its signs from British Sign Language and uses them to convey language between deaf-blind people and others. The hands of one are used on the hands and body of another to relay language and to communicate. I have taken my learning and studying and used hands-on signing to soothe babies when distressed. The results have been very positive.

I first used hands-on signing with Blossom when she was just a few weeks old. I instinctively felt she would like it and that she would respond well to it, and she did. I have gone on to use this technique as part of my research. All the babies have enjoyed the use of hands-on signing and have benefited from the experience of positive touch combined with a soothing tone.

When, at eight months, Blossom appeared upset (after relocating her to her own bedroom) I used the signs taken from British Sign Language and placed my hands on to Blossom's chest and torso to sign the following, 'calm', 'calm', 'patience', 'calm'. 'Patience', 'patience', 'calm', 'calm'. 'Relax', 'relax', 'relax'. I repeated these actions until Blossom was soothed. I spoke the words aloud while simultaneously signing on her body. She was soothed by both the action (therefore the contact we shared) and the tone of my voice. I repeatedly performed these movements on Blossom's chest and torso until she appeared calm and relaxed.

If I say these words to Blossom now I see her ears prick up, she appears alert and her body moves in response to my words. She is immediately aware of my words and the soothing tone of my voice. When Blossom was four years old, I asked her what this meant to her and she said: 'I don't know.' We all recognise her response and have wondered what she experiences internally by the use of these words now. When Blossom was a little older I made further enquiries and asked her what she feels in her body. She said she gets 'a tickly feeling' in her tummy. I was delighted by her response and interested to know more. I was pleased to hear how she was so attuned to her own body and that she could readily find the words to describe her bodily feelings. For now, I am fully satisfied that the sensation experienced in Blossom's 'tummy' is a body-held memory of our early contact. If you think about Blossom's experience at eight months, I imagine the 'tickly feeling' in her tummy holds both negative and positive body-held memories.

Signing in Action

In the images overleaf I am demonstrating how I used some of the signs of British Sign Language to soothe and calm baby Sebastian in his distress. You can see that at the beginning Sebastian was tearful and as we worked through this exercise Sebastian was calmed and soothed by the experience. Cat, his mother, was interested in how these actions would soothe him and she was keen to learn how to use the techniques.

You can see in the second image how we have captured Sebastian's distress, and simply by using my hands-on signing, and mirroring his distress and using 'ooowwaa, ooowwaa' vocal expressions (by me) followed by smiling by his mum, we have soothed him in his distress. He was totally engrossed by our expressions both verbally and non-verbally.

In the third picture, which was taken just moments after the second, I am smiling at Sebastian's curiosity

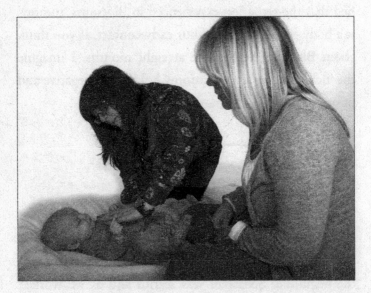

Using hands-on signing with baby Sebastian in his distress

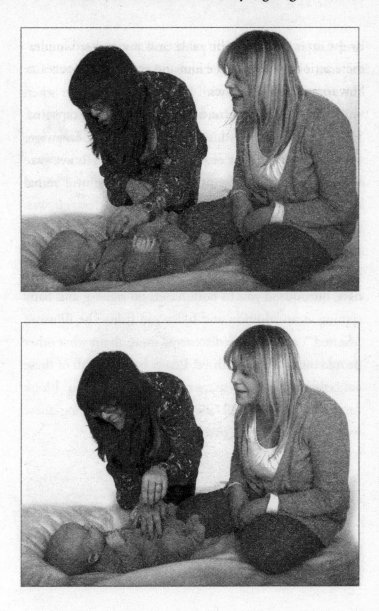

and Cat is smiling with pride and joy at her wonderful son. I am still using hands-on signing to teach Cat the system that I used with Blossom to soothe her when she was tearful. Sebastian began to vocalise at this point. He 'spoke' with both his voice and his body language. He smiled with an air of positive curiosity. His eye-gaze was towards me and he gurgled in his delightful verbal expressions.

In this chapter I have shown the many benefits of transitioning from The Blossom Method™ to baby signing. I have introduced you to both hands-on signing and baby signing as an addition and follow-on from The Blossom Method™, and we have discovered more about what other people think about all three! I truly believe in all of these concepts and want to share my passion with you. I look forward to hearing all about your success using these wonderful non-verbal parenting tools.

Good Luck!

This book has emphasised the value of **observing, mirroring** and **responding** to your baby's body language and facial expressions. I hope you will have become more skilled in your understanding in relation to the world of the non-verbal and that your efforts have been rewarded by a closer understanding of your baby and a mutual sense of understanding and being understood.

As your child grows and develops, your opportunities for communication will be enhanced through the use of verbal and non-verbal methods. The Blossom Method™ of observing, mirroring and responding will have shown you how to talk and how to listen. As your relationship develops over the years your methods will change, but by observing, understanding and responding to your child's needs you will be able to support him and communicate effectively with him throughout his life.

Resources

Useful organisations and websites

Babies Can Sign
Yorkshire-based baby-signing company that runs classes across the region.
www.babiescansign.co.uk

Baby Signing Mummy
A website to discover and explore the world of baby signing. Includes information, class details and resources.
www.babysigningmummy.com

Brain Insights
An American-based website focusing on the value of early contact, communication and play in the brain development of babies and young children.
www.braininsightsonline.com

British-Sign.co.uk

A range of British Sign Language resources, including free information and study guides.

www.british-sign.co.uk

DeafBooks

A range of British Sign Language books and resources in the LET'S SIGN Series, including many free downloads.

www.deafbooks.co.uk; 01642 674298

Inspired Children

A programme offering life skills for kids from Dr Rosina McAlpine, an Australian-based parenting expert, author and radio presenter.

www.inspiredchildren.com

National Deaf Children's Society

Help and support for families and professionals working/ living with deaf children.

www.ndcs.org.uk; 020 7490 8656

Sign2Music

Baby-signing company in Northern Ireland that facilitates programmes for all children supporting communication, bonding and development.

www.sign2music.co.uk

TinyTalk
The biggest baby-signing classes organisation in the UK and Ireland.
www.tinytalk.co.uk; 01483 301444

Useful parenting books

Atkins, Sue, *Parenting Made Easy* (Vermilion, 2012)

Burnside, Annie, *Soul to Soul Parenting* (Wyatt-MacKenzie Publishing, 2010)

Ekman, Paul, *Emotions Revealed: Understanding Faces and Feelings* (Phoenix, 2004)

Ekman, Paul, *Why Kids Lie: How Parents Can Encourage Truthfulness* (Penguin, 1989)

Gerhardt, Sue, *Why Love Matters* (Routledge, 2004)

Gordon, Dr Yehudi, *Birth and Beyond* (Vermilion, 2002)

Grace, Janey Lee, *Imperfectly Natural Woman* (Crown House Publishing, 2006)

Hogg, Tracy, and Blau, Melinda, *Secrets of the Baby Whisperer* (Vermilion, 2001)

Liedloff, Jean, *The Continuum Concept* (Perseus, 1998)

McAlpine, Rosina (Ed.), *Inspired Children: How the Leading Minds of Today Raise Their Kids* (Darlington Press, 2011)

McGhee, Christina, *Parenting Apart* (Vermilion, 2011)

McNelis, Deborah, *Love Your Baby* (Brain Insights, 2008)

Miller, Alice, *The Truth Will Set You Free* (Perseus, 2001)

Mongon, Marie F., *HypnoBirthing* (River Tree, 1992)

Northrup, Dr Christiane, *Women's Bodies, Women's Wisdom* (Piatkus, 1995)

Rapley, Gill, and Murkett, Tracey, *Baby-led Weaning* (Vermilion, 2008)

Richards, Naomi, *The Parent's Toolkit* (Vermilion, 2012)

Roberts, Janette, *Healthy Parents, Healthy Baby* (Random House, 2012)

Sansone, Antonella, *Mothers, Babies and their Body Language* (Karnac, 2004)

Wilson, Alan, *How To be a Parent Champion* (Develop Your Child CIC, 2011)

Winnicot, D.W., *The Child, the Family and the Outside World* (Penguin, 1964)

Index

Note: page numbers in italic refer to illustrations or photographs

Acknowledgements

The inspiration for this book has grown from my experience of being in relationships: in relationship with myself and others, as a daughter, partner, mother, stepmother, psychotherapist, client, supervisor, friend and sibling. The understanding and acceptance of my own history, my mother's deafness and the acknowledgement of the gifts this has brought have inspired me further in the writing of this book.

Mum, thank you for all of your support and encouragement. Vuyo, thank you for your love and support. A special thank you to you, Blossom, our wonderful daughter – you are my shining star. I love you to the moon and back. Your enthusiasm for sharing our story is amazing.

I would like to acknowledge Dr Rosina McAlpine. You are an inspiration to me.

Thank you to Lydia Noor, George Bassett and Dr Linda

Finlay, inspirational clinicians from ScPTI.

Thank you to Jennifer M. Hatfield, MHS, CCC/SLP Speech Language Pathologist and President, for writing the inspirational foreword to this book. Thank you to Consultant Psychiatrist Dr Haraldur Erlendsson, a truly innovative clinician who has inspired and enhanced my psychotherapeutic practice.

There are three further clinicians I wish personally to thank and pay tribute to: Pauline Brumwell, Alison Dowdeswell and Andrew Enever.

A special thank you goes to Nyasha Mutavayi and Viki Jones – also Integrative Psychotherapists in advanced training at ScPTI. Without your love and friendship my life would feel less.

Thank you to Jenni Moulson, Ashley, Liz, Sheila, Nicole, John Nicholls and Paula Lister Nicholls, and Emma Hammond. A special thank you to all of my research participants in the UK, USA and Canada.

Thank you to one and all.

About the Author

Vivien Sabel is a UKCP Relational Psychotherapist, clinical supervisor, baby expert and mother. She is fluent in British Sign Language and formerly trained and registered as a Trainee BSL Interpreter.

http://www.viviensabel.com/
http://viviensabel68.blogspot.com